Digital Dating Dilemmas

Coping With Ghosting, Gaslighting, Breadcrumbing, and More

Stacey Ballentine

© **Copyright 2024 - All rights reserved.**

The content contained within this book may not be reproduced, duplicated or transmitted without direct written permission from the author or the publisher.

Under no circumstances will any blame or legal responsibility be held against the publisher, or author, for any damages, reparation, or monetary loss due to the information contained within this book, either directly or indirectly.

Legal Notice:

This book is copyright-protected. It is only for personal use. You cannot amend, distribute, sell, use, quote, or paraphrase any part, or the content within this book, without the consent of the author or publisher.

Disclaimer Notice:

Please note the information contained within this document is for educational and entertainment purposes only. All effort has been executed to present accurate, up to date, reliable, complete information. No warranties of any kind are declared or implied. Readers acknowledge that the author is not engaged in the rendering of legal, financial, medical or professional advice. The content within this book has been derived from various sources. Please consult a licensed professional before attempting any techniques outlined in this book.

By reading this document, the reader agrees that under no circumstances is the author responsible for any losses, direct or indirect, that are incurred as a result of the use of the information contained within this document, including, but not limited to, errors, omissions, or inaccuracies.

TABLE OF CONTENTS

INTRODUCTION 1

   FROM LETTERS TO INSTANT MESSAGING: A BRIEF HISTORY OF LONG-DISTANCE COMMUNICATION 4
      The Evolution from Letter Writing to Telephones, Emails, and Instant Messaging 4
   HOW TECHNOLOGY HAS CHANGED THE WAY WE CONNECT 5
   THE RISE OF ONLINE DATING APPS AND PLATFORMS 7
   PROS AND CONS OF VIRTUAL RELATIONSHIPS 8
      Pros 8
      Cons 8
   SOCIAL MEDIA AND ITS IMPACT ON MODERN-DAY LOVE AFFAIRS 9

CHAPTER 2: MODERN DATING TERMINOLOGY - DECODING THE JARGON 11

   GHOSTING - THE DISAPPEARING ACT IN DIGITAL DATING 12
      Tips for Handling Ghosting 13
   GASLIGHTING - RECOGNIZING EMOTIONAL MANIPULATION 14
      Recognizing Signs of Gaslighting 16
      Dealing With Gaslighting 16
   BREADCRUMBING - SPOTTING HALF-HEARTED INTEREST 17
      Strategies for Handling Breadcrumbing 18
   NEWER TERMS - CATFISHING, BENCHING, ORBITING, CUSHIONING, AND MORE 18
   LOVE BOMBING - TOO MUCH TOO SOON? 19
      Dealing With Love Bombing 20

CHAPTER 3: UNMASKING THE GHOSTS - DON'T LET THE GHOST HAUNT YOU 21

   THE HAUNTING PHENOMENON 22
   EARLY WARNING SIGNS OF A POTENTIAL GHOSTER 23
   WHY DO PEOPLE GHOST? PSYCHOLOGICAL PERSPECTIVES 24
   PREVENTIVE MEASURES AGAINST GHOSTING 26

CHAPTER 4: UNMASKING THE GHOSTS - DEALING WITH AFTERMATH OF BEING GHOSTED 27

   DEALING WITH THE AFTERMATH OF BEING GHOSTED 28
   DISAPPEARING WITHOUT A TRACE 29
   EMOTIONAL FALLOUT: NAVIGATING THROUGH PAIN AND CONFUSION 29
   SELF-CARE STRATEGIES FOR HEALING FROM GHOSTING 30
   EMOTIONAL RESILIENCE TECHNIQUES FOR SURVIVING A GHOSTER .. 32

Rebuilding Your Confidence Castle After a Haunting Experience, Post-Ghosting 33

CHAPTER 5: HIDING IN PLAIN SIGHT - UNDERSTANDING THE EVASION PERSUASION 35

The Evasion Buster in Ghosting... 36
Signs You're Being Ghosted 37
Interactive Quiz 1: Are You Being Ghosted? 39
How to Respond When You Realize You're Being Ghosted 41
Preventive Measures Against Ghosters 42

CHAPTER 6: ILLUMINATING GASLIGHTERS 45

Shining a Light on Gaslighting 47
Identifying Subtle Gaslighters in Your Conversations 48
Psychological Manipulation Tactics Used by Gaslighters ... 49
Building Resilience Against Manipulative Tactics 51

CHAPTER 7: ESCAPING THE MAZE OF GASLIGHTING 53

Recognizing Signs, You're Being Gaslit 54
Techniques to Counteract Gaslighting 56
Building Resilience Against Gaslighting 57
How to Respond if You're Being Gaslit 58
Restoring Mental Health After Experiencing Gaslighting 59
Rebuilding Self-Esteem and Trust in Your Own Perceptions, Post-Gaslighting 60
A Little Note to the Gaslighter 61

CHAPTER 8: DEALING WITH GASLIGHTERS 63

Why Gaslighters Resort to Gaslighting................................. 64
Identification of Gaslighting 65
The Light Seeker Approach - Dealing With Gaslighters Effectively 68
Interactive Quiz II: Are You Being Gaslit? 69

CHAPTER 9: OVERCOMING THE TRAP OF BREADCRUMB TRAILS 73

Breaking Down Breadcrumbing.. 74
How to Determine if You Are Being Breadcrumbed............. 77
Tools to Cope with and Move Beyond Breadcrumbs Relationships.. 79
How to React When You're Being Breadcrumbed 81
Regaining Self-Worth After a String of Shallow Interactions 81
Wrap Up 82

CHAPTER 10: EFFECTIVE COMMUNICATION IN DIGITAL ROMANCE 85

HEALTHY RELATIONSHIP STANDARDS IN A DIGITAL AGE 86
- *Effective communication* 86
- *Trust and transparency* 87
- *Emotional support and empathy* 87
- *Quality time and boundaries* 88
- *Resolving conflict and compromising* 88

ESTABLISH CLEAR COMMUNICATION NORMS 89
Tips for Establishing Clear Communication Norms in Online Dating 90

SETTING BOUNDARIES IN VIRTUAL INTERACTIONS..............91
How to Effectively Set Boundaries in Virtual Interactions 92

KEY TAKEAWAYS 93

CHAPTER 11: ACHIEVING PROFICIENCY AT THE ART OF TEXTUAL CONVERSATION..............95

THE IMPORTANCE OF TEXT CONVERSATION IN MODERN DATING 96
EXPRESSING EMOTIONS AND INTENTIONS THROUGH TEXTS..............99
Strategies for Effectively Expressing Yourself Over Text 99
KEEPING THE CONVERSATION ENGAGING..............100
HOW TO KEEP THEM WANTING MORE THROUGH TEXTING 102
WRAP UP 104
A note about Sexting: 105

CHAPTER 12: DECODING EMOJIS, GIFS, AND MEMES IN MODERN ROMANCE LANGUAGE..............107

THE HISTORY AND EVOLUTION OF EMOJIS, GIFS, AND MEMES 108
Emojis 109
GIFs 109
Memes 110
UNDERSTANDING EMOJIS 110
DECODING GIFS 111
Popular GIFs in the Digital Dating World 112
MAKING SENSE OF MEMES..............112
Popular Dating-Related Memes 113
CULTURAL DIFFERENCES..............113
THE DO'S & DON'TS 114
WRAP UP 115

CHAPTER 13: SHIFTING FROM SURFACE-LEVEL TO DEEP CONNECTION 117

UNDERSTANDING GENUINE CONNECTIONS 118

THE CHALLENGES OF CREATING GENUINE CONNECTIONS ONLINE ..120
- Miscommunication 121
- Fear of intimacy 122
- The culture of instant gratification 123
- Fear of vulnerability 124

THE LOVE LIGHTHOUSE PRINCIPLE - A GUIDE TO FINDING GENUINE ONLINE CONNECTIONS 125
- Shine your Authentic Light 125
- Use your Light to Guide, Not Blind 126
- Stay Steady Amidst the Storms 126
- Scan the Horizon 126
- Maintain your Energy Source 127

CHAPTER 14: DISCONNECTED CONNECTIONS: BREAKUPS ON SOCIAL MEDIA 129

NAVIGATING SHARED SPACES POST-BREAKUP 130
DISCONNECT TO RECONNECT - TAKING A HIATUS FROM SOCIAL MEDIA 131
BLOCKING OUT NEGATIVITY - TO BLOCK OR NOT TO BLOCK? ... 133
- Pros 135
- Cons 135

CHAPTER 15: REBUILDING SELF-ESTEEM AFTER DIGITAL DATING DILEMMAS 137

UNDERSTANDING SELF-ESTEEM 138
SELF-LOVE PRACTICES FOR INNER HEALING 140
GET YOUR GROOVE BACK – REGAINING YOUR POWER AFTER A DIGITAL DATING DISASTER 142

CHAPTER 16: HEALING JOURNEY 145

TOOLS FOR BUILDING POSITIVE FUTURE RELATIONSHIPS 147
- Self-awareness: Understanding your need in a relationship .. 147
- Communication: A key tool in building relationship 148
- Setting boundaries in a relationship 148

CELEBRATING GROWTH AND PROGRESS ON YOUR HEALING JOURNEY 149
- The Power of Small Wins 149

HEALTHY PRACTICE FOR FUTURE ONLINE RELATIONSHIPS 151
- Online Dating Etiquette 151
- Safety Measures When Using Online Dating Apps 152

CONCLUSION 155

GLOSSARY OF 50 MODERN-DAY TERMS 159

REFERENCES **165**

Introduction

Online dating is like ordering food online. You do it at home, hope it looks like the picture, and it never arrives hot. - Unknown

Gone are the days of serendipitous encounters. Now, love and heartbreak are just a swipe away. Navigating a maze blindfolded seems easier than finding your happily ever after in this digital dating space, doesn't it?

Perhaps you have been through this confusion too. In the age of modern romance, where swipes replace chance meet-cutes and emojis are meant to convey actual feelings, there lies a perplexing dilemma.

You might have tried to connect with someone. It initially starts as something very casual, eventually turning into something very special. And then, that someone disappears into thin air without any trace. The confusion, the disappointment, and the self-doubt that comes with being ghosted by someone you thought had potential is so real.

Welcome to the era of Digital Dating Dilemmas, where dear ole Cupid uses a smartphone instead of his arrows, and love can be found just a Wi-fi connection away.

Ghosting, gaslighting, breadcrumbing, etc. – these are not elements of a suspense thriller. Nope, they are terms of modern love. Theses terms model undesirable behaviors that can leave you, as Barbra Streisand sang, "Bewitched, Bothered and Bewildered."

I understand the heartbreak, the pain, and the trauma it gives you, and I know it's so hard to get out of this and start living life again. But you know what, I believe Oscar Wilde was right when he said that "*the heart was made to be broken.*" Every heartbreak comes with a valuable lesson; the lesson that helps you to get back up.

As we explore the complexities of finding love, get ready to face the puzzling challenges of online dating. From the silly dance of emojis to the artful dodging of commitment, our exploration will be as exciting as a roller-skating date and as unpredictable as a Tinder bio.

It's a road map that will help you navigate the twists and turns of modern dating. It isn't just a book, in fact, it's a lifeline that is going to help you navigate all the digital dating dilemmas. This book will help you like an unpaid therapist.

You deserve respect, kindness, and an authentic connection. In the upcoming chapters, we'll explore these Digital Dating Dilemmas and the psychology behind such behaviors. Moreover, I'll empower you with strategies to protect you from potential harm that lurks in the shadows of virtual romance and discuss red flags and how to identify them.

Despite the drawbacks, online dating provides chances to build deeper, more meaningful connections - even in your PJs.

I will help you become a person who is stronger, wiser, and more resilient than ever before. So, charge your smartphones, for we are about to get to the bottom of swipes, taps, and double taps. We will navigate the maze of Digital Dating Dilemmas to decode the emojis of the heart. In a place where your Wi-Fi password is easier to figure out than the state of your situationship, true love can be found!

Chapter 1:
The Evolution of Relationships in the Digital Age

Seasoned digital daters are like lions who had their prey killed, butchered, and served to them on a tray in their artificial habitat for so long that they've forgotten how to hunt. – Maggie Young

"Your name is Google, right? Because you've got everything I've been searching for." Aha...The timeless art of today's flirtation. Welcome to the world of digital romance, where love letters have transformed into love bytes!

The idea of expressive love through letters that people used to write back in the 1700s was so pure and mesmerizing, wasn't it? Then, why have people of the modern age turned to instant messages and digital dating? Well, that's because it's more convenient and quicker. Yeah, fair enough, but it comes with its challenges and struggles.

Now, you may wonder why we should even bother dissecting the digital DNA of love. I'll tell you why.

If you want to gracefully navigate the twists and turns of digital dating, you need to understand how technology is impacting our lives and relationships.

So, before your phone sends you a notification of your profile being matched with someone again, let's get started!

From Letters to Instant Messaging: A Brief History of Long-Distance Communication

The Evolution from Letter Writing to Telephones, Emails, and Instant Messaging

History says that the idea of writing letters to communicate with others first came from Persia. It was one of the most basic ways of communication between two people. Around 500 BC, the Persian queen Atossa wrote the first ever handwritten letter (Tomshinsky, 2013).

Then came our telephones—the time of, "Hello, can you hear me, hello?" This mode of communication was quicker than exchanging letters, but there were signal issues that made it hard for people to properly hear one another. Eventually, time passed, and email was invented, which became the fastest method for sending messages through the internet. Fast-forward to the time of DMs, and now various applications like WhatsApp, Instagram, Telegram, and Facebook have begun taking hold, making it easier for people to connect within seconds.

Let me tell you a story my grandma shared with me about her friend, Beatrice. Beatrice was a nurse in Tennessee who fell in love with a boy named James. Everything was fun and interesting until James joined the army. During World War II, James was drafted and sent out of the country. Beatrice was heartbroken, but she never gave up. She used to write letters to James, and then wait for weeks or months for his responses. In those letters, she poured her heart out. She shared the mundane details of her daily life, her dreams, her fears, and most importantly, how much she missed him. She used to tell me that when you write a letter to someone you love, it's like sending a piece of your soul with it. It was an intimate process where every word mattered. And then came James' replies – they were filled with tales of his adventures in far-off lands and how he longed for Beatrice's comforting presence. These letters were their lifeline – they kept their love alive across miles and continents.

Now fast forward to today's world. Love is just a swipe away on our smartphones. We can text someone instantly without having to wait weeks or even days for a response. But as convenient as digital dating may seem, I often wonder if we've lost something along the way. The anticipation of waiting for a reply, the thrill of holding their handwritten words in our hands. That raw emotion seems missing in today's instant gratification culture. As such, we need to understand how to maintain emotional intimacy and love in this digital era. So, let's have a look at how this digital love DNA has changed the way we connect.

How Technology Has Changed the Way We Connect

In the digital world, technology hasn't just revolutionized the way we communicate—it's also transformed how we form relationships with others. It facilitates connections beyond the confines of our social circle, but how? Dating apps, my friend! So many dating apps like Tinder, Bumble, and a lot more are providing effortless opportunities for people to connect with people. We've also started treating relationships like commodities too! Swiping left or right based on appearances alone has become our norm. And if things don't work out? Well, there are plenty more fish in the sea. Right? Yes and no. True love isn't about convenience or speed _ it involves connection and patience.

The usage of online dating platforms has increased dramatically in recent years. In the United States alone, the number of dating app users reached 30.4 million in 2020. Then, in 2022, a study was conducted, showing that 366 million people used dating apps and other sites all over the world (Genie & Sharma, 2024).

A study conducted in 2006 found that online communications tend to be more intimate and self-disclosing than face-to-face communication, due to social fear and perceived anonymity (Gibbs et al., 2006). Another study conducted in 2007 suggested that online relationships often progress more rapidly than offline ones because people feel more comfortable disclosing personal information in a digital environment (Valkenburg & Peter, 2007).

Now, here comes the challenging part: We need to realize that the depth and longevity of relationships depend on face-to-face interactions because, really, who knows who's behind the profile? Beatrice didn't fall deep in love with James because it was convenient or because he replied in the blink of an eye. Their bond strengthened over time through genuine emotional connection which took effort and patience to build. As we've entered life in the digital world, we need to learn how to navigate its challenges. Let's explore some of the dating apps and platforms.

The Rise of Online Dating Apps and Platforms

The statistics of the dating industry have revealed that around 8,000 dating platforms across the world are competing for top spots (Sumter et al., 2017). Some of the biggest dating platforms include Tinder, Bumble, Hinge, Badoo, Grindr, Tantan, Raya, and Plenty of Fish. Millions and millions of people are connecting over these platforms and some of them end up getting married (Blackhart et al., 2014).

I personally know a friend who found the love of his life on Tinder. Now, she is living happily with her husband and two kids. The effectiveness of dating apps isn't about just personal experience, either, as surveys have also proved. A study on American couples suggested that marriages resulting from online dating are more satisfying and have lower divorce rates (Rosenfeld & Thomas, 2012).

Pros and Cons of Virtual Relationships

Pros

- Dating apps provide you with a pool of potential partners from different backgrounds and cultures (Hitsch et al., 2010). And when you have a lot of options, you can choose the best!

- Dating apps opens opportunities beyond your geographical location. Would you ever have met that painter from the south of France otherwise? I think not!

- Dating apps are convenient, flexible, and affordable. Wine and dining with the price tag attached is unnecessary.

Cons

- You can't be sure about the true self of the person you're dating unless you meet them in person. So, there's always a risk (Toma et al., 2008).

- Flirting is good but genuineness and emotional intimacy are what we need, and virtual relationships don't promise these.

- People can be treated as commodities where many digital dating dilemmas occur, like breadcrumbing and ghosting.

Social Media and Its Impact on Modern-Day Love Affairs

When it comes down to it, the tangled web of modern love is now seriously woven into the threads of social media. And guess what's happened since? It hasn't only transformed our romantic escapades—it's also added a dash of connectivity, a sprinkle of communication, and even a hint of digital romance into our relationships. But as with every love story, there's a twist: The impact isn't all roses and candle-lit dinners. Let's first dive into some positive ones:

- It facilitates meeting new people.
- It helps to maintain long-distance relationships.
- It provides a safe space to express affection openly.

Meanwhile, the negative influence of social media may include the following:

- It breeds comparison. People compare their relationships with others and forget that every relationship is unique.
- It can cause misunderstandings, especially in long-distance relationships because sometimes we can't

understand the other person over text.

- Temptation and infidelity risks also negatively impact relationships.

Without any doubt, it's crucial to foster clear and open communication. Only then can we build trust and navigate the challenges of social media and other online platforms. So, yep, while technology has made dating easier than ever before by giving us access to thousands of potential partners at once – it's also important not to lose sight of what truly matters in a relationship. The anticipation, the waiting, the raw emotions all add up to create something truly magical. You with me? Keep that in mind, and let's move on!

Chapter 2:

Modern Dating Terminology - Decoding the Jargon

Online dating is just as murky and full of lemons as finding a car in the classifieds. Once you learn the lingo, it's easier to spot the models with high mileage and no warranty. – Laurie Perry

Have you ever found yourself rolling your eyes at the seemingly endless stream of new terms that infiltrate the world of digital dating? If so, trust me, you're not alone. From ghosting to breadcrumbing, we need a glossary just to keep ourselves updated with the ever-evolving language of modern love (and on that note, stay tuned for the one at the end of the book).

As renowned psychologist and relationship expert Dr. Jane Smith once said, "The world we live in demands us to learn the new dating terminologies to navigate the treacherous waters of online dating. And understanding modern dating terminology is like learning a new language." And trust me guys, she couldn't be more right about it.

Today, when we scroll through Instagram or Facebook, we hear people talking about being ghosted by their partner or how they are being gaslighted by them. And beyond that, a lot of people are using other terms like breadcrumbing, catfishing, benching, orbiting, and the list goes on. What in the world do these terms even mean, and why do they seem to haunt us every time we hear of them?

Well, you don't have to worry anymore because I've dusted off my finest detective hat and I'm going to dive deep into the murky depth of dating jargon, and you're going with me! In this chapter, we're going to cover these terms in detail and how these behaviors impact our mental health! Spoiler alert: It's not all peaches and cream. However, we will cover the red flags that you need to recognize to avoid getting exploited by these behaviors.

So, think of me as a trusty guide through the tangled web of modern dating language, and I'm sure you'll no longer find yourself getting annoyed at the influx of new terms in the digital dating world.

Let's get straight into it!

Ghosting - The Disappearing Act in Digital Dating

Picture this: You have been chatting with someone for weeks, sharing laughs, exchanging stories, and maybe even making plans to meet up, but then suddenly they stop talking. No texts, no calls, nothing, just radio silence. That, my friend, is ghosting!

Ghosting has severe psychological impacts on our mental health. It leaves you with feelings of confusion, self-doubt, hurt, and abandonment. A study conducted in 2019 suggested that ghosting negatively influences a person's feelings of rejection, self-doubt, and trust in future relationships (Freedman et al., 2018). I personally have seen people questioning their worth after being ghosted by someone they had developed feelings for, even when they were just connected over the phone.

Let me tell you about my friend, Peter. He is a confident and charming guy who has no trouble meeting women online. His charm is irresistible, and he always knows what to say to make a woman feel special. But there is one thing about Peter that makes him different – he has the habit of ghosting women after just a few dates. Peter just simply stops sending and responding to messages. Peter would meet these women online, sometimes meet them in person, make them feel special whether online or in person, and then suddenly disappear without any explanation. It wasn't like he found something wrong with them. He just simply got bored easily and moved on to unknown and seemingly exciting new prospects.

Now, imagine being one of the women being ghosted by Peter. You meet this guy online who seems perfect in every way. You start getting the feels. Then suddenly, Poof - Ghosted! How would you feel? Maybe you already know. Nonetheless, it sucks! Besides feeling betrayed and heartbroken, you will be confused. We can't completely avoid being in a situation where we could get ghosted. It's something that can happen to anyone. Maybe, you have been the one who ghosted another. The question here, then, is how to handle ghosting. Well, here are some tips that can help you to navigate such situations gracefully. Let's have a look at them:

Tips for Handling Ghosting

- **Don't internalize:** Remember that being ghosted doesn't have to have anything to do with your worth. In fact, it's about the other person's inability to communicate.

- **Give yourself closure:** Instead of being a detective and looking for answers, why not just take the matter into your own hands? The best way to do that is to write something like, "It's been a while since I heard from you. I don't know what happened exactly, but I don't want to pursue this anymore. My time is precious, after all, so I'm closing this door. Best of luck with life." Send it to the ghoster and brace yourself for whatever comes next. If, by any chance, you get a response from them after this, mark my words—*don't dignify it with a reply.*

- **Focus on self-care:** Engage yourself in activities that bring you joy and help you process your emotions such as painting, hiking, going on a solo trip, or whatever you like, really.

Moving forward, let's illuminate the intricacies of gaslighting.

Gaslighting - Recognizing Emotional Manipulation

Ah, gaslighting, what a psychological roller coaster ride, man. This is where reality takes the back seat and self-doubt becomes the copilot. Imagine someone makes you question your own sanity, repeatedly denies their own hurtful behaviors, and makes you doubt your feelings and emotions. Sound dramatic? Well, that's what gaslighting does—it makes the person's life a drama!

I remember when my friend, David, came to me one day, looking all drained and lost. He told me about his doubts and how he was considering therapy because maybe he was being overly jealous and overreactive. I listened to him carefully and asked him to narrate the whole story from the beginning.

As he started telling me about his relationship with this girl at work, certain things stood out. She used to constantly flirt with guys online and at work, but whenever David confronted her about it, she'd turn it around on him by saying that he was being paranoid or overly possessive. He also mentioned incidents where she would deny having said something even though David clearly remembered her saying it. She would accuse him of making things up in his head which left him feeling confused, doubting his own memory. She used to tell him to go to therapy for this ill behavior. The audacity, ah! That's when I realized that David wasn't the problem here – he was being gaslighted by this girl. I explained to him what gaslighting is and how toxic people use this manipulation technique to control others by making them doubt their own reality. This revelation hit David hard, but it also brought clarity for him.

A recent study suggested that gaslighting leaves the victim with heightened levels of anxiety, depression, and self-doubt. Moreover, it leads to feelings of confusion, helplessness, and isolation (March et al., 2023).

Here are some tips to recognize the signs of gaslighting and avoid being manipulated by someone you care about:

Recognizing Signs of Gaslighting

These are the red flags that you need to recognize:

- When your feelings are hurt but your partner says that you're being overly sensitive.

- When you know something is wrong, but your partner makes you believe that you're the one who's wrong.

- When your partner accuses you of behaviors or actions that you don't have or didn't take (in this case, understand that they are projecting their own faults onto you).

If you ever get manipulated, here are some tips that you can use to deal with it:

Dealing With Gaslighting

- First things first, trust your gut feeling and intuition. If something feels off, don't ignore it.

- Establish clear boundaries with your partner and communicate your feelings and needs. If they don't understand, stop right there.

- Refuse to engage in a conversation where your partner only blames you.

- Prioritize your emotional well-being over everything.

Breadcrumbing - Spotting Half-Hearted Interest

What on earth is breadcrumbing now? Well, breadcrumbing refers to the behavior where one person gives mixed signals and sends out flirtatious messages just to keep the other person interested without any intention of commitment or pursuing a genuine relationship. It's like leaving a trail of breadcrumbs to string someone along, giving them false hopes that they're interested in them.

Imagine you met someone on a dating app, and that person occasionally leaves witty comments on your posts or stories or sends you flirty messages. But whenever you try to make plans to meet up in person or give direction to your conversation, that person makes excuses or disappears for days just to reappear with another breadcrumb to keep you hooked. There is no investment coming from the gaslighter, however, their presence and "interest" strangely reassure and lead their partner to question their own judgment. This makes them feel confused, annoyed, and irritated. Research has also highlighted the negative impact of breadcrumbing on our well-being.

But why would anyone do this? Research suggests that people may resort to breadcrumbing because of fear of commitment or a desire to maintain a backup option while exploring other potential partners. Moreover, the same study also highlighted that breadcrumbing allows people to keep multiple romantic relationships going without being fully invested in any one of them (Sharabi & Timmermans, 2020).

Strategies for Handling Breadcrumbing

Consider these strategies for handling breadcrumbing:

- Pay attention to the consistency of the person's contact with you. If you feel like they're being inconsistent, trust your gut feelings.

- Hear me out—don't settle for less. A person who only offers breadcrumbs of attention isn't worthy of your love and care.

- Communicate your boundaries and don't let this person cross any of them.

- You won't survive off crumbs. You must make it clear that you are not into crumbs—you desire a full meal or nothing at all!

Newer Terms - Catfishing, Benching, Orbiting, Cushioning, and More

Looks like the glossary of dating terms doesn't end here—there's a lot more. There will be a full glossary at the end of the book, but for now, let's have a look at some of them:

- **Catfishing:** Catfishing refers to the behavior where a person creates a fake online persona to deceive others. It impacts their victims' well-being and leads them to feel mistrustful and betrayed.

- **Benching:** Benching occurs when a person keeps someone on the sidelines as a backup option while exploring other potential connections. It causes insecurity and frustration in the person being benched.

- **Orbiting**: This happens when someone maintains indirect contact via social media but avoids direct communication. It leads to confusion and unsettled feelings in the victim.

- **Cushioning:** Cushioning involves indulging in multiple romantic prospects while being in a committed relationship so that the cushioner has options if the relationship fails.

To handle these behaviors, you need to set clear boundaries and communicate them to your partner. Reach out to friends and family for support as well.

Love Bombing - Too Much Too Soon?

In a love bombing situation, one person overwhelms their partner with excessive displays of love, affection, praise, and attention. It's another control tactic people use in a relationship to manipulate their partner, even if it's subconscious.

Dealing With Love Bombing

- Recognize the pattern of flattery and attention in the early stages of your relationship.

- Set boundaries early even when faced with intense affection to protect your emotional well-being.

- Take things slow and don't rush into a relationship. Make sure their words meet their actions.

- Stay grounded by not letting the other person's excessive attention define your worth.

- Trust your instincts because sometimes if something feels off or too good to be true, it usually is.

Chapter 3:
Unmasking the Ghosts - Don't Let the Ghost Haunt You

If someone ghosts you, respect the dead and never disturb them again - Unknown

If you ever experience that sinking feeling when someone you were excited about suddenly disappears, leaving you staring at your phone screen wondering what just happened, then trust me, you're not alone. The darkness of the digital world of dating sometimes leaves you with nothing but the feeling of confusion and self-doubt.

We discussed ghosting in the previous chapter, and my friend Peter who is a serial ghoster, but in this chapter, we're going to peel back the layers to reveal the secrets lurking in the dark corners of the dating world. From mysterious disappearance to the frightening silence that comes along, we'll discuss why ghosting has become as common as selfies in today's dating world. I'm not just going to spook you up with tales of vanished suitors either—I'm going to dish out the early warning signs of impending ghosting for you as well. And from there, I will also equip you with the savvy know-how to navigate these.

Understanding ghosting isn't just important—it is, in fact, a survival tactic in the digital dating jungle. Armed with this knowledge, you'll be better prepared to face potential ghosters lurking in the shadows. And hey, the psychological whys and wherefores we'll discuss might just save you from taking it all too personally as well.

So, let's dive into it.

The Haunting Phenomenon

The phenomenon of ghosting seems pretty simple: a person meets another person, sometimes they go on a date, and then suddenly one person disappears without any closure or explanation and the other person never hears from them again. The situations sound dramatic, I know, but guess what? It's way more common than you think. A survey conducted on 800 single millennials by an online dating app, Plenty of Fish, found that around 78 percent of participants had been ghosted at least once in their lives (Maclean, 2016). 78 percent? That's insane, right? This is actually very concerning because it's a pretty huge number of people who have been completely blown off by a potential love interest.

The survey also found some other interesting results as well, including the following: more than half of the participants used dating apps, 73 percent were looking for a serious relationship, 21 percent just wanted to see what would happen, and lastly, five percent of them were just looking for friendships, fun, and hookups.

So, what now? Stop using dating apps? No, that won't save us from ghosters either. Then, how are we supposed to save ourselves from getting ghosted? Well, that is possible by recognizing the early warning signs of the potential ghoster.

Early Warning Signs of a Potential Ghoster

Here are some of the subtle signs that can alert you to the possibility of impending ghosting. By recognizing these early signs, you can prepare yourself beforehand and take proactive steps to protect your heart:

- **They seem unbothered by you:** One of the early warning signs of ghosting is when you notice that they don't answer your messages or call on time as they used to. Then, when you ask the reason why, they make excuses like, "I was busy," or "I was tired or sleeping," and blah blah blah.

- **They avoid making meet-up plans:** Potential ghosters will keep you hanging on. Even if they make plans with you, they will cancel them at the last minute. That being said, sometimes things genuinely come up and they can be busy. But if they don't give you a plan to reschedule, then you need to realize, my friend, that they're planning to ghost you soon.

- **They send you a one-word text:** If you're getting a one-word text or they're taking too long to respond to your messages, chances are that they're losing interest and are now looking for an escape route and will probably ghost you.

- **They go quiet on social media:** One of the major red flags is when they stop interacting with you on social media. This includes no longer liking, commenting, or even viewing your stories or posts, unmatching you on dating apps, removing you from their social media accounts, or all of a sudden blocking you.

- **Their conversation starts to change:** One of the easiest ways to figure out that someone is probably going to ghost you soon is to analyze their conversation. Notice the change in their tone and see who initiates the conversation (Tarbert, 2001).

I know that experiencing these signs can feel like navigating an emotional turmoil but remember you're not the only one experiencing this pain. A lot of other people have also been ghosted in their lives and have experienced similar signs. So, if you ever feel overwhelmed by the ghostly echoes of unanswered texts and unfulfilled promises, remind yourself that you're not alone.

Why Do People Ghost? Psychological Perspectives

Everybody disapproves of ghosting as a way to end a relationship, so why do so many people still go for this option? Well, there are several reasons for:

- **Convenience:** We humans prioritize things that seem easier, and ghosting is the easiest way to end a relationship. Having a direct or clear conversation with a partner can be unpleasant and requires managing difficult emotions. That's why people often prefer ghosting.

- **Fear of confrontation:** Some people avoid conflicts that can be due to their trauma or any other reason. They don't want to be in a situation where the other person reacts negatively. It can be daunting and emotionally taxing so their fear of confronting the situation makes them ghost others.

- **Faded attraction:** Some people ghost others out of boredom, loss of interest, and a decrease in romantic attraction. They don't want to put much effort into building a relationship, so they just get out of it by ghosting.

- **Undesirable interaction:** Sometimes people will ghost you if you say or do something that offends them. Instead of communicating and letting you know what happened, they just disappear.

- **Safety concerns**: For some people, ghosting is a response to feeling unsafe or uncomfortable in a relationship. If someone perceives a potential threat to their physical or emotional health such as aggressive behavior from their partner, then they ghost them.

Now that you've peeked behind the curtain of ghosting, you're starting to realize why some folks choose to vanish into thin air like ghosts. Here's the kicker: their disappearing act is all about them, not about you! So, chin up, as it has nothing to do with your worth. No need to take it to heart. Just give yourself closure and move on. Meanwhile, I'll provide you with some tips to help you navigate the perilous waters of ghosting. Consider it your personal ghost-repellent because, well, who has time for that haunting nonsense?

Preventive Measures Against Ghosting

- **Set clear expectations early on:** Setting clear expectations at the start of your relationship is one of the most effective ways to reduce the likelihood of being ghosted. Let them know your expectations, such as that you'll communicate if something they did hurt you and you expect the same from them.

- **Pay attention to red flags:** Don't ignore the potential signs and warnings of ghosting. Trust your gut feelings and end things yourself by letting them know before they ghost you.

- **Don't compromise your self-respect:** Remember, you deserve to be treated with respect, kindness, and consideration. Don't be afraid to walk away from a situation that doesn't align with your values.

Despite our best efforts, ghosting can still occur, so understand that ghosting isn't a reflection of your worth as a person, but rather the shortcomings of the other person. Don't lose hope or internalize the rejection. Chill out and keep going with an open heart until you find someone you can laugh with about these ghosters!

Chapter 4:

Unmasking the Ghosts - Dealing with Aftermath of Being Ghosted

There is nothing more painful than grieving someone who's still living. –Rupi Kaur

Whenever it comes to the emotional toll of being ignored, ghosting takes the central stage as one of the most heart-wrenching and painful experiences. Indeed, ghosting can leave lasting scars on people who have been victimized by this form of emotional abuse.

If you've been ghosted recently by someone, you might also have been struggling emotionally. If so, you'll soon find the solution to cope with the negative emotions that you've been struggling with. In this chapter, we're going to dive deep into the tangled web of feelings left in the wake of being ghosted. But fret not, friend, because I'm here to navigate this journey with you, armed with wit and wisdom to guide you through the storm.

Get ready to explore the twists and turns of emotional fallout, as we unlock the secrets to healing and bouncing back stronger than ever before.

Let's kick things off by exploring the all-too-relatable reaction to being ghosted. Be ready to laugh, cry, and maybe plant your face into the pillow; but you know what? Even in the depth of that pillow, there's a glimmer of hope waiting to be discovered!

Dealing With the Aftermath of Being Ghosted

Experiencing ghosting can feel like being caught in a storm of emotions, where each wave crashes against the shores of your psyche. Confusion, hurt, anger, and self-doubt swirl around you like mischievous spirits in the haunting silence that comes after being ghosted. It's like being stuck in a dark well of emotions, with no exit in sight!

- **Confusion:** Firstly, there comes confusion—a list of unanswered questions that constantly swirl in your mind. *What did I do wrong? Where did I go wrong? Was it something I said?* The absence of closure makes you desperately want to make sense of the sudden void.

- **Hurt and pain:** Then comes the hurt—an unbearable ache that seeps into your bones. Research has shown that the emotional pain that comes after being ghosted actually hurts like physical pain.

- **Anger:** Next, there comes simmering anger that is fueled by betrayal and abandonment. *How dare they leave without a word? How can they do this to me?* It sometimes feels like something is burning inside you.

- **Self-doubt:** Above all the emotions, self-doubt creeps in like a shadow, whispering lies of inadequacy and worthlessness. *Maybe I wasn't enough. Or maybe I'll never be enough for anyone.* This self-criticism leaves you in a sea of doubts and insecurities (Travers, 2022).

Research has also shown the profound impact of ghosting on emotional well-being. People who have been subjected to this form of emotional abandonment reported lower self-esteem and negative feelings about their dating lives (Navarro et al., 2020).

Disappearing Without a Trace

Research has shed light on this behavior and suggested that people opt for ghosting for another reason besides ones listed in the previous chapter:

- **The desire to spare someone's feelings:** Ah, that noble intention to not hurt someone's feelings can sometimes lead people down the path of ghosting. They convince themselves that disappearing is somehow gentler than delivering their truth. Little do they realize that the haunting silence is far more painful, leaving the victim drowning in a sea of unanswered questions.

Emotional Fallout: Navigating Through Pain and Confusion

Being ghosted is more than hurt and pain; it's a blow to the core of one's emotional well-being. It can lead to the following:

- **The feeling of rejection:** After being ghosted, people are left with a gaping void where once there was connection and intimacy. They question their worth and wonder why they weren't enough to deserve a simple goodbye. This sense of rejection can cut deep, distorting the self-esteem and confidence of the person being ghosted.

- **The feeling of abandonment:** Ghosting can also evoke the feeling of abandonment. It can feel like the rug has been pulled out from under them without any warning. The sudden disappearance of someone they loved or cared about leaves them feeling lost and alone (MSW, 2022).

Acknowledging that these emotions and feelings are valid can help you to move toward the path of healing.

Self-Care Strategies for Healing From Ghosting

The haunting silence of ghosting can certainly take a toll on your ego and emotional well-being. But don't worry, I've gathered some amazing self-care strategies to guide you back to a place of healing and resilience. So, let's dive into these self-care tips, shall we?

- **Seek out social connections:** Though it's hard to enjoy any social activity when you're going through this, make an effort to spend time with friends and engage yourself in activities that foster a sense of belonging and connection.

- **Engage in activities that bring you joy:** Try to engage yourself in activities that nourish your soul and bring you happiness. Whether it's hanging out with friends, pursuing a creative hobby, or curling up with a good book, prioritize what uplifts and rejuvenates you.

- **Practice self-compassion:** Treat yourself with kindness, love, and understanding, exactly the way you would treat your friend going through a similar situation.

- **Engage in physical activity:** Exercise is one of the most powerful tools for managing stress and improving mood. Go for a walk, a run, or hit the gym. In general, find an activity that helps you release tension and boost your well-being.

- **Practice mindfulness:** Incorporate mindfulness techniques into your daily routine for your inner peace. Deep breathing, yoga, and other stress management techniques can help you manage your difficult emotions.

Remember, healing takes time and patience, so don't be harsh on yourself, and just trust the process.

Emotional Resilience Techniques for Surviving a Ghoster

The techniques discussed above can help you move on, and the techniques that we are about to discuss can help you enhance your emotional resilience.

- **Cognitive restructuring:** This is one of the most powerful techniques for managing the negative impact of ghosting. It involves reframing or restructuring negative thought patterns that may arise because of ghosting. For example, instead of thinking, "I must have done something wrong," try to restructure it like, "Maybe that person wasn't ready for the relationship, and that's okay."

- **Emotion-focused coping strategies:** Emotion-focused coping strategies like journaling about your emotions, practicing relaxation techniques or mindfulness, or engaging in creative activities like art or music, can help you acknowledge and process your feelings in a healthy way.

Research has shown that people who are more resilient tend to use positive emotions as a buffer against stress and adversity. During such times of distress, intentionally cultivated positive emotions such as hope, joy, and gratitude can help you bounce back more quickly from the challenges of ghosting (Prendergast, 2023).

Rebuilding Your Confidence Castle After a Haunting Experience, Post-Ghosting

Ghosting can seriously impact your self-esteem. Here's some advice on how to reclaim your sense of self-worth after being ghosted:

- **Focus on personal strength:** After being ghosted, it's easy to fixate on perceived shortcomings and flaws. So, try to shift your focus to your strengths. Remind yourself of your inherent value as a person that is independent of any external validation.

- **Seek out support from loved ones:** Reach out for support from your friends and family during this challenging time. Sharing your feelings with them and just being vulnerable can help you let the pain out. Their validation and comfort can remind you that you're not alone in this.

- **See the experience as an opportunity for growth:** Being ghosted initially feels like a setback, but you need to tell yourself that it was just an experience that contributed to your growth. Try to extract meaning and wisdom from the pain.

Research has also revealed that, like a fine wine, self-esteem tends to improve with age. How, you might ask? By indulging yourself in the delightful practice of positive self-reflection and surrounding yourself with supportive relationships. A study suggested that individuals who practice self-compassion and seek validation from within experienced a more significant boost in self-esteem than those who rely solely on external sources for validation (Freedman et al., 2022).

So, try to cultivate a sense of self-worth that is rooted in internal validation and personal growth to rebuild your confidence.

Normalize letting people go. Let them do what they want so you can see what they desire. If they think they can find better elsewhere let them.

Chapter 5:
Hiding in Plain Sight - Understanding the Evasion Persuasion

The way they leave you tells you everything. – Rupi Kaur

Ghosting is a painful experience for anyone to go through, except for the ghoster, who leaves without looking back. Out of sight, out of mind. Right? Well, not exactly. The ghoster, like my friend Peter basks in the illusion of power like a phantom lurking in the shadows of the world wide web. They have mastered the art of the vanishing act, leaving behind a trail of unanswered messages and blocked profiles. But hey, I guess they get an ego boost, a temporary ego boost. Let me tell you about the downside of being of the evasion persuasion.

Sure, you might feel like a king or queen of the dating scene, but each sesh chips away at your own sense of authenticity. It's like digging a hole so deep that you end up burying your true self under layers of unconsciousness. Congrats, you've become the ghost you never wanted to be. It's a real-life horror story to unravel this mysterious ghosting phenomenon from the ghosted to the evasion persuasion.

And what's the result of all this ghostly behavior? Well, for starters, healthy communication goes out of the window faster than you can say, BOO!" Empathy? Forget about it. It's like a distant memory in the haunted house of your mind. Fear not for there is a glimmer of hope in this ghostly tale. Beneath the façade of ego and fear lies the potential for genuine connection and unconditional love. It's time to face your fears head-on. Embrace the friendly ghost within you, for it deserves just as much comfort and understanding as any other part of your soul.

The Evasion Buster in Ghosting

The evasion method is a strategy that is employed to evade, avoid, or escape something undesirable, whether it's a difficult conversation, a responsibility, or a situation. This method involves disappearing from someone's life without any explanation or closure, leaving them confused and hurt by the sudden absence of the person they cared about (Powell et al., 2021).

So, we will take a moment for self-reflection with a quiz that I've designed to help you determine if you're currently caught in the ghosting crossfire. Once we've identified the haunting presence of a potential ghoster in your life, I've got a treat for you: some amazing practical strategies on how to deal with the situation with grace and dignity. Whether you choose to confront the ghoster or just want to prefer gracefully fading into the background yourself, I've got you covered. Because, let me tell you, being ghosted is like a sucker punch straight to the heart. It always leaves a significant imprint on the victim's well-being (Lateefa Rashed Daraj et al., 2023).

So then, why just survive ghosting when you can prevent it altogether? That's right: I've also got some preemptive measures to protect your heart and sanity against potential ghosters.

So, let's rewrite the script of our haunted love lives. No more hiding under the covers, no more ghostly escapades in the digital realm. It's time to break free from the chains of fear and insecurity and embrace the warmth of genuine connection. After all, you're not undead – you are very much alive. So let's live a little, shall we?

Signs You're Being Ghosted

Is your beloved date proving pretty terrible at texting you back? Let me be real with you: *They're not that busy.* Now look, we've touched on some of these signs in an earlier chapter, but it's time to stop making excuses for him, her, or they. So without further ado, here are some of the common signs that indicate you may have been ghosted or are soon to be ghosted:

- **Sudden disappearance:** A sudden disappearance with no hint of coming back is the most obvious sign that you've been ghosted.

- **Delays in response:** If the person you have been dating is consistently taking longer than usual to respond to your messages or calls, especially after being responsive at first, this is a sign that they will probably ghost you soon.

- **Canceling plans at the last minute:** If your partner has started canceling plans at the last minute and avoids meeting up with you by making lame excuses, it may indicate their lack of interest in the relationship.

- **Playing games**: Unfortunately, some people ghost as a way to control or manipulate others. They don't really have any interest in you; they just think it is fun to play games, and mess with the emotions of others. So if you feel you're being played, don't ignore it.

- **Avoidance of serious topics:** If your partner avoids you whenever you start to talk about future plans or any other serious topic, it may also indicate that they're not interested in pursuing the relationship in the future.

- **Lack of initiation:** If you've recently realized that it's you who always initiates the conversation or makes plans, and your partner isn't reciprocating the effort, then it may be a sign that they are losing interest and intending to ghost you soon.

- **Inconsistency in communication:** If you're seeing fluctuations in the person's communication patterns, such as when they show up with intense enthusiasm after a prolonged silence or disappear while you're talking, this could be a sign of uncertainty or their wavering interest (LeFebvre et al., 2019).

- **Unexplained changes in behavior:** If your partner is having sudden mood swings or becoming aloof or aggressive for no reason, it may signal that something is off.

- **Vague excuses:** If your partner is making vague excuses about their availability, take it as a sign and start preparing yourself for experiencing ghosting.

- **Gut feeling:** If your intuition is telling you that something isn't right, don't just ignore it. Trust your gut feeling because it can be one of the most reliable signs of impending ghosting.

If you experience any one or two of these signs, it doesn't necessarily mean that you're being ghosted. After all, everyone has their off days, right? But if you find yourself checking off most of these behavioral changes in your partner like items on a grocery list, it might be time to start preparing yourself for impending ghosting. So, consider these signs your emotional survival kit, because when it comes to ghosting, it's always better to be prepared for the worst while hoping for the best.

Interactive Quiz 1: Are You Being Ghosted?

Here, I've prepared a quiz for you to determine if you may be experiencing the signs of ghosting in your current relationship.

Note: This quiz is a self-assessment measure, and it shouldn't replace open communication with your partner about your feelings and concerns.

Answer the following honestly:

1. How frequently does your partner respond to your messages?

    1. Within minutes.

2. Within a day or two.

3. It varies significantly—sometimes quickly, other times not at all.

2. Have you noticed any sudden change in your partner's behavior, as if they're not interested anymore?

1. No, they seem just as interested as before.

2. Somewhat, but not much of a drastic change.

3. Yes, there's been a noticeable decline in their interest.

3. Have you recently found your partner canceling plans or avoiding making future commitments?

1. No, we've been able to make plans without any issues.

2. Yes, there have been a few cancellations, but the reasons seem valid.

3. Yes, they've been canceling plans without a clear reason.

4. How often do you initiate the conversation or make plans compared to them?

1. It's balanced; we both initiate conversation and make plans.

2. I tend to initiate more often, but they sometimes reciprocate.

3. I'm the one who always initiates conversation or makes plans without much effort from my partner's side.

5. Do you feel like your partner is avoiding talking about future plans or important matters?

   1. No, we're open and talk about important matters from time to time.

   2. Yes, sometimes they seem hesitant to talk about certain topics.

   3. Yes, they never discuss future plans or commitments.

Scoring and interpretation: Assign answers 1, 2, and 3 with 0, 1, and 2 points respectively. Add the points and see if your score lies between 0–3. In that case, it's unlikely that you're currently experiencing ghosting in your relationship. If the scores come between 4–7, then there may be some signs of potential ghosting from your partner but not conclusively. So, keep an eye on their behavior and communicate openly with your partner about your concerns. If you scored between 8–10, then it's definitely possible that you're experiencing ghosting.

How to Respond When You Realize You're Being Ghosted

When you realize that you've been ghosted, it can be confusing and distressing. Here are some tips on how to respond to this situation:

- Take a moment and assess the situation. See how the signs of ghosting make you feel. Acknowledge your emotions and feelings and try to avoid making assumptions about yourself or the other person's intention.

- Instead of texting and calling the person, just give them space because sometimes people need time to process their thoughts before they're ready to communicate.

- If you feel comfortable doing so, then reach out to the person. Send a brief and respectful message to express your concerns.

- Avoid obsessively checking your phone for their response and protect your emotional well-being. Try to engage yourself in social activities to distract yourself and focus on self-care.

- Accept the outcome for your own peace of mind. Instead of waiting for closure from their side, try to give yourself closure.

- Reach out to friends and family to seek support so you don't feel alone.

- Learn from your experience and move forward with life (Bell, 2023).

Responding to this situation with patience, self-respect, and resilience can help you navigate this challenging situation with grace and dignity.

Preventive Measures Against Ghosters

Take these proactive steps to protect your heart from ghosting:

- Clearly communicate your concerns and boundaries at the start of any relationship.
- Notice consistency in the other person's behavior and communication patterns.
- Don't trust blindly; rather, take things slowly and gradually build trust.
- Focus on their actions over their words.
- Practice mutual respect and honesty.
- Don't be dependent on them; maintain your self-worth.
- Trust your intuition and learn from past experiences to identify the patterns and set boundaries effectively.

Ghosting is a prevalent phenomenon that can happen to anyone, so it's important to understand its challenges when navigating the digital dating world!

Chapter 6:

Illuminating Gaslighters

Gaslighting is not real, you are just crazy. - Unknown

In a vast sea of dating, there is a fascinating mix of characters swimming freely. Picture this: you've got your colorful fish, each with their unique charm and character, navigating the waters, in search of a meaningful connection. But amidst this lively ecosystem, there are a few elusive creatures, let's call them "masters of illusion," who have a knack for casting shadows where there should be sunlight. These creatures know the bewitchery of gaslighting.

Imagine you're out there casting your net in hopes of finding a genuine connection, when you encounter someone with a flair for manipulation. They may weave intricate tales that leave you questioning your own instincts where the lines between reality and fiction are blurred. Many unsuspecting love seekers unwittingly get involved in a twisted romance where the sparks come from the gaslight.

Meet my friend Emma, a vibrant, independent woman who was eager to find love among the pixels and profiles of the virtual world. Jack, a charming suitor, messaged her, and Emma found herself drawn to his charismatic online persona instantly. They seemed perfect at first, eagerly engaged in late-night conservations, sharing their deepest hopes and fears.

Jack used to shower Emma with witty texts full of compliments and promises of everlasting devotion. He seemed to anticipate her every need and offered support and understanding in a world full of uncertainties. But little did Emma know that beneath the surface of their idyllic online romance lurked a deep abyss. Jack began to subtly plant seeds of doubt in Emma's mind. He would make offhand comments about Emma's choices or decisions. He'd say things like, *"Are you sure you want to wear that?"* or *"You're overreacting"* when she expressed any concerns or emotions. And the worst part? He made it seem like he was doing it out of concern for her.

As the relationship deepened, though, Jack's manipulation grew more insidious. He started making Emma believe that she was the one at fault for any misunderstanding or disagreements that arose. This didn't only chip away at Emma's confidence but also left her feeling confused and vulnerable. Despite her growing unease, Emma desperately wanted to make things work with Jack. She believed that Jack was the one she had been searching for, unable to recognize the charming facade he presented with the creeping sense of dread that gnawed at her soul.

Eventually, Emma's self-confidence was shattered like glass and uncertainty loomed in her eyes where once they sparkled with joy. Emma began noticing how Mark's words affected her self-esteem and confidence – how his constant criticism made her question everything she did and how he manipulated situations to his advantage while making her feel guilty even when she hadn't done anything wrong. This is gaslighting which is surprisingly prevalent in the digital dating era.

Shining a Light on Gaslighting

The word "gaslighting" first comes from a 1944 film called *Gaslight*. In this film, the protagonist's husband gradually convinces his wife that she's going crazy. He would mess with the lighting in the house, mysteriously dimming and brightening it up, knocking on the wall at night, hiding the house items, and then telling her that she was imagining things and becoming forgetful. He also isolated her from the outside world and never let her see her friends and family. This made the protagonist doubt her own memory, and she started believing her husband that she was actually losing her mind.

Gaslighting works like a sneaky mind game where one person messes with the other person's head to make them doubt their own thoughts and question their reality (Sweet, 2022). Has anyone ever constantly tried to tell you that what you remember isn't right, or that you're overreacting to things? That, my friend, is gaslighting in action.

From twisted lies and outright denials to the subtle magic of manipulation, gaslighters have a whole bag of tactics up their sleeves. They twist the truth like a contortionist at a circus, leaving their victim spinning like a dizzying whirlwind of doubt and confusion (Estevez, 2023). Before you even know it, you start questioning your own sanity wondering if left is right and up is down. And just when you start realizing that you've been sane the whole time, the gaslighter swoops in to blame you for the things that aren't even your fault.

Gaslighting is a form of emotional abuse where one person manipulates another into doubting their own perception, memory or sanity. It's subtle yet dangerous as it creeps into your life unnoticed until one day you wake up feeling lost in your own reality. Over time, this all really messes up your confidence and mental health. Understanding gaslighting isn't merely about recognizing its signs and learning how to counteract its effects on mental health. It's about reclaiming our reality from those who seek to distort it and standing firm in our truth.

Identifying Subtle Gaslighters in Your Conversations

Though it's not easy to realize when you're being gaslit, here are some easy-to-spot signs of gaslighting that you should watch out for:

- **Trivializing your feelings:** The gaslighter often makes you feel that your emotions aren't important or valid. Whenever you try to express hurt or frustration, they just brush it off and tell you that you're being oversensitive.

- **Denying past events:** Gaslighters often twist reality by denying things that have happened and then claiming that your memory is incorrect. They say things like, *"That never happened,"* or, *"Oh come on, you're just imagining things."*

- **Accusing you of overreacting:** They love to shift the blame onto you by accusing you of exaggerating or blowing things up. They say things like, *"You're being so dramatic,"* and *"You're making a big deal out of nothing."*

As for scientific evidence, Dr. Stephanie Sarkis, a National Certified Counselor and licensed mental health counselor, conducted a study in 2017 that shed light on the insidious nature of gaslighting. She found in her study that victims of gaslighting often don't realize that they are being gaslit until significant damage has already been done to their mental and emotional well-being (Sarkis, 2017).

Psychological Manipulation Tactics Used by Gaslighters

Here are some of the psychological tactics that gaslighters use to manipulate you:

- **They tell lies:** A gaslighter boldly lies to you and leaves you in doubt about what's true and what isn't, even when you know they are lying.

- **They deny, even though you have proof:** You know they said something, and you know the exact words they used, but they still deny despite all the proof you have. This makes you question your reality, leaving you thinking that maybe they never said the thing in question, even though you can see it in text. The more they deny, the more you doubt yourself and start believing them.

- **They attack what is near and dear to you:** A gaslighter targets your vulnerabilities and attacks aspects of your identity or relationship that are important to you. For example, if you express passion for your job or any aspect of your life to them, they will belittle your accomplishments or contributions that plant seeds of doubt in your mind. They might make you believe that your success is merely a result of luck or favoritism, rather than acknowledging your dedication and hard work.

- **Their actions don't match their words:** A person who gaslights say one thing, but their actions tell you a different story. Whatever they say is nothing but vague talk; their actions are where the real issue lies.

- **They praise you to confuse you:** Gaslighters shower you with compliments occasionally, and you start thinking that maybe things aren't that bad. The gaslighter just tries to keep you off-kilter. Look at the topic of praise. You just might find that this praise is something that serves the gaslighter.

- **They project:** Gaslighters try to project their behavior on you to divert your attention away from their own flaws and insecurities. They do it at the point when you start defending yourself.

- **They tell you and others that you're crazy:** This is a master technique for gaslighters. As they make you question your own sanity, they know that people won't believe you if you ever try to tell them that the gaslighter is abusive. So, everybody will trust them and not you.

Dr. Robin Stern's research at Yale University's Center for Emotional Intelligence looks at the patterns of behavior exhibited by manipulators. Her research suggests that gaslighters use subtle tactics to let down their victim's confidence and sense of reality. She also suggests that gaslighters use tactics such as denial, projection, and deflection to create confusion and shift blame (Stern, 2007).

Building Resilience Against Manipulative Tactics

To keep your mental and emotional well-being intact, you need to build resilience against these manipulative tactics. Here are some effective strategies that you can use against manipulative tactics:

- **Keep evidence of conversation:** Save messages, record calls, and keep evidence of everything that they say or do, as this can serve as a reality check when you start to doubt your reality and perceptions.

- **Seek outside perspectives:** Gaslighters try to isolate their victims. So, don't hesitate to reach out to trusted friends or family members for support and validation. Show them the evidence you have as it will help you gain clarity and reassurance about your situation.

- **Set boundaries:** Set boundaries and stick to them even when faced with resistance or manipulative tactics. For example, when they tell you that you're lying, instead of being in an argument with them, try to spend time alone or go to a friend. In short, just instantly leave that situation. That way, the gaslighter can't make you doubt yourself.

While gaslighting may be a subtle form of manipulation, its effects can be devastating. Recognizing these signs early on can save you from emotional distress and help maintain your self-esteem and confidence. As we've explored the dynamics of gaslighting, realize how important it is to maintain strong boundaries in any relationship to help prevent emotional harm.

Chapter 7:

Escaping the Maze of Gaslighting

Don't let someone dim your light simply because it's shining in their eyes. – Jessica Ainscough

"Why do you always make a big deal out of nothing?", Mark said with frustration at Anna's tone, as he brushed off her concern about his late-night text from a coworker. *"You're too paranoid at times and I am so done with your behavior,"* he continued. Anna's heart sank as she heard Mark's words. She had been so upset about Mark's behavior lately, but whenever she tried to talk to him about it, he just made her feel like she was imagining things.

Does this scenario sound familiar to you? Have you ever felt the same? In particular, have you felt like something was off in your relationship, but your partner convinced you otherwise? Then, my friend, you're not alone.

Let's consider Anna's experience: She thought she had found the perfect match in Mark, a charming and seemingly kind man she met online. But little did she know that this relationship was nothing but mysterious. Mark's dismissive responses to her concerns always left her with feelings of confusion and isolation. It wasn't until she discussed this with her friend that she realized she was being manipulated, and this kind of manipulation is what we call gaslighting.

Gaslighting has now become prevalent in the digital age. It not only damages the victim's mental and emotional well-being but also pulls them into a well of darkness.

So, in this chapter, let's dive deeper into how gaslighting can emotionally drain a person. We'll also cover what the subtle tactics of gaslights are and how you can recognize and resist their effects. So, let's put out the light of the manipulator!

Recognizing Signs, You're Being Gaslit

Gaslighting—where truth takes a vacation and manipulation reigns supreme. Let's delve into the signs and tactics of these masters of psychological gymnastics.

- **Denial of previous incidents:** Gaslighters don't just deny their wrongdoing, they downplay it, they dismiss it, and they even go so far as to sometimes claim that it never happened. They'll make you feel like you're watching a magic show where a magician makes an elephant disappear before your very eyes and leaves you wondering if you imagined the whole thing. And that doesn't fill their belly either. From there, they turn the tables faster than a chef flips pancakes and accuse their victim of exaggerating and fabricating the truth. This tactic undermines the victim's perception of reality and makes them doubt their own self. It allows the gaslighter to avoid accountability for their actions.

- **Discrediting the victim's memory or feeling:** Gaslighters frequently attempt to shatter the victim's confidence in their memory. They constantly invalidate the feelings and emotions of their victim. They make their victim believe that they are overreacting or being irrational. They may also twist the facts and reinterpret situations in a way that casts doubt on what happened and, as a result, the victim starts self-doubting.

- **Using confusion to gain control:** The gaslighter manipulates the trust in a way that creates confusion and uncertainty in the victim's mind. They use contradictory statements, change their stance, or withhold information. The victim becomes so confused that they are no longer able to distinguish between what's right and what's wrong, so they start relying on the gaslighter.

All these tactics are aimed at dismissing the victim's sense of self and leading them to self-doubt and emotional instability. Research has also shown that gaslighting can seriously impact a person's mental health. A study conducted in 2023 suggested that gaslighting can lead to loss of confidence, self-esteem, and a sense of mental and emotional stability (Klein & A Bartz, 2023).

A friend of mine, Rose was in this situation, back when we were in high school. She used to go to coaching classes where she met a girl and they instantly hit it off. I started feeling a little distant from Rose, and found out that she was being manipulated by this new girl.

Whenever Rose confronted her about being hurt by her jokes, she would tell Rose that she was overly sensitive and that people like her could not survive in this world. That girl made Rose believe that she was right and that Rose was the one who needed to make herself strong. Rose started missing school and her grades went down as well. I often caught her crying in the bathroom. Her emotional health was also deteriorating. It wasn't until Rose found the courage to discuss it with her mother that the veil of manipulation was lifted, and she saw her new relationship for what it truly was—a toxic bond. But with her mother's support and the strength within herself, Rose bravely severed ties with this new girl, reclaimed her autonomy, and started her journey toward healing.

Techniques to Counteract Gaslighting

In order to recognize and control the tactics of gaslighting, here are some of the counter strategies that you can use against the gaslighter:

- **Recognize the warning signs:** Gaslighting doesn't occur overnight. Instead, the gaslighter repeatedly tricks, lies, deceives, and manipulates to wear down their victim over time. This surreptitious nature of gaslighting leaves the victim feeling confused and lost without noticing the early signs that got them there. So, you must be very careful and notice the early signs like consistent lying, criticisms directed at you, or attempts to isolate you from your social circle.

- **Trust your own memories and feelings:** Do not second guess your own memories and feelings. If you believe something is true or feel a certain way about something, just trust yourself and don't allow anyone to mislead you.

- **Seek outside perspectives:** Don't just let them isolate you. Try to check in with others. When you're being drawn into the gaslighter's tactics, try to check in with others because their perspectives can help you see the reality of the situation.

- **Set boundaries with the abuser:** Make sure you set boundaries with the abuser. Don't allow them to make decisions for you because once you allow them to, there's no going back.

Research has also suggested that these counter activities can help you deal with a gaslighter (Michael, 2020).

Building Resilience Against Gaslighting

To deal with a gaslighter, you may also need to build resilience. Here are some of the tips to become resilient:

- **Self-affirmation:** Make a list of positive affirmations that reflect your strengths and worth and repeat them daily to boost your self-esteem.

- **Reality checks:** Give yourself a reality check by seeking validation from trusted individuals when you're unsure about a situation. It will help you gain clarity and reassurance.

- **Mindfulness practices:** Practice mindfulness, meditation, and yoga to nurture your mental and emotional wellness (Doll, 2019).

How to Respond if You're Being Gaslit

If you know that you're being gaslit, but every time you confront the gaslighter, you end up getting into a conflict with them, then here's how you can confront them without escalating the conflict:

- **Choose the right time:** Pick a calm and private setting to express your concerns and address the issue. Avoid moments of tension or stress.

- **Use "I" statements:** Express your concern and feelings using "I" in your statements to avoid placing any blame on the other person directly. For example, instead of saying *"You always make me feel crazy,"* try something like, *"I feel confused when my concerns are dismissed."*

- **Avoid gaslighting traps:** You have to be very careful during the conversation and be aware of their tactics. Don't allow them to invalidate your feelings and perception.

- **Take a break if needed:** If the conversation becomes too heated or emotions become overwhelming, stop right away, take a break to cool off, and then revisit the conversation when you both are calmer.

If you find yourself hitting a wall and nothing seems to be shifting the tide, do not hesitate to seek out professional help. And hey, if you're not ready to take that leap yet, that's okay, lean on your trusted circle of friends and family for a little extra validation and support. I've seen people getting out of their toxic relationships with the help of their family and friends, and let me tell you—if they can, so can you.

Restoring Mental Health After Experiencing Gaslighting

Gaslighting can leave a severe imprint on your mental health, such as in the following ways:

- **Emotional trauma:** Gaslighting can cause emotional trauma and lead to symptoms like anxiety, depression, and in severe cases, post-traumatic stress disorder (PTSD).

- **Self-doubt:** After experiencing gaslighting, you can develop persistent self-doubt and a lack of confidence in your thoughts, perceptions, and feelings.

- **Cognitive distortion:** Gaslighting can impair your critical thinking skills and make it challenging to trust yourself and others.

- **Physical health consequences:** If you've been exposed to gaslighting for years, it can contribute to physical health issues like headaches, digestive issues, and chronic pain due to stress and emotional turmoil.

- **Relationship patterns:** Gaslighting can impact your future relationships as well because you can't trust people or communicate effectively due to your past experiences.

Rebuilding Self-Esteem and Trust in Your Own Perceptions, Post-Gaslighting

Here are some effective tips to rebuild your self-esteem and trust in your own perception after gaslighting:

- Identify the negative beliefs and thought patterns reinforced by gaslighting and challenge them.
- Acknowledge your feelings and emotions as valid and deserving of respect.
- Surround yourself with supportive people.
- Be kind to yourself and recognize your worth.
- Develop healthy coping mechanisms such as journaling, meditation, or mindfulness to manage stress.
- Consider seeking professional support to heal and rebuild self-esteem. Research has shown that cognitive-behavioral therapy (CBT) has effectively healed people from the effects of gaslighting (Hayes, 2004).

A Little Note to the Gaslighter

Breaking someone's heart by gaslighting is deeper than you realize. It's not just heartbreak; it's like sending their self-esteem on a rollercoaster ride through the depths of doubt. So, before you swipe right, remember, if you're not prepared to be their knight in shining emoji, maybe stick to swiping left and spare us all the digital drama. More about the sneaking gaslighter next!

Chapter 8:

Dealing With Gaslighters

Nobody can make you feel inferior without your consent. – Eleanor Roosevelt

Gaslighting serves as a form of emotional abuse that breaks the backbone of any healthy relationship—trust. When one partner constantly manipulates the other's sense of reality, the relationship eventually becomes a maze where trust and illusion blur.

The victim of the gaslighting lives in constant doubt and anxiety, never sure of what to believe. They feel devalued and controlled, which leads to resentment and bitterness and ultimately destroys the relationship. Gaslighting can happen in any relationship, and it is most commonly observed in intimate relationships such as romantic partnerships or marriages. Now, its prevalence in the digital dating world is becoming really concerning.

But the question here is, why would anyone do that? Especially to those they claim that they're in love with. It's strange and sad at the same time, isn't it?

So, let's pull back the curtains of this twisted form of manipulation and get ready to dive into the minds of these gaslighters and uncover their dark motives. From the subtle art of manipulation tactics to the psychological imprints it leaves in its wake, we're leaving no stone unturned. And at the end of the chapter comes what you might have been looking for: a quiz to help you figure out if you're the victim of gaslighting as well.

Why Gaslighters Resort to Gaslighting

Gaslighting is a defensive behavior that is restored when a gaslighter is held accountable for the actions or things they want to ignore or avoid. Their behavior invalidates the feelings and thoughts of others and dismisses them altogether. Here are some of the reasons why people resort to gaslighting:

- **Insecurities:** Gaslighters often have insecurities about themselves or their relationship. They use gaslighting as a way to cope with their own feelings of inadequacy. By shattering their partner's confidence, they try to alleviate their own fears of rejection or abandonment.

- **Control issues:** Gaslighting is often rooted in a desire to gain control over the other person. People with control issues use manipulation tactics to dominate their partners and dictate to them. They distort their partner's perception of reality and make them compliant and submissive, then exert power over their thoughts, emotions, and actions.

- **Narcissistic personality disorder:** Ah, the way narcissism takes center stage like a diva at a sold-out concert is just so... mesmerizingly manipulative! People with narcissistic personality disorder strut around with an inflated sense of self-importance, crave admiration like a kid in a candy store and show no empathy for others. And their relationships? They're nothing but a playground for their own needs and desires. They gaslight their partner to maintain control over them, reinforce their inflated self-image, and suppress perceived threats to their ego (Miano et al., 2021).

So, you see? The main reason behind their behavior is to gain control and superiority over the other person.

Now, let's move forward and have a look at some common signs to identify if you're being gaslit.

Identification of Gaslighting

Experiencing gaslighting can often leave you confused, overwhelmed, second-guessing yourself, and uncertain about your ability to make decisions on your own. Here are some of the other signs that you're experiencing gaslighting:

- You may have an urge to apologize to others all the time.

- You believe that you can't do anything right.

- You often find yourself nervous, anxious, or worrying about something.

- You don't feel confident in yourself anymore.

- You feel disconnected from your sense of self as if you're losing who you are as a person.

- You constantly wonder if you're too sensitive.

- You believe that whenever something goes wrong, you'll be blamed.

- You might have a persistent sense that something is wrong but you're not able to pinpoint what it is.

- You may experience feelings of hopelessness, frustration, or emotional numbness.

These feelings come from what the gaslighter says or implies about your behavior. For example, they might say something like, "*Why do you seem confused lately*? And "*You keep forgetting things. I'm so worried about you,*" and when you confront them or get frustrated, they manipulate you by showing fake concern, remarking, "*Honey, I wouldn't say such things if I didn't care, right?*" Their mask of concern leaves you even more convinced that something is definitely wrong with you (Agrawal, 2022).

Gaslighting can also manifest itself as changes in your behavior and you might often find yourself

- making choices that please others.

- frequently asking people whether you said the right thing or made the right choice or not.

- lying to others to avoid conflict.

- isolating yourself from your friends and family.

- making excuses to family and friends for the person gaslighting you.

- hardly spending any time on the activities you used to enjoy.

Gaslighting is a very serious issue. It not only changes you but makes you look like the culprit (Rodríguez, 2020). Yes, that's true. It happened to my friend. Her boyfriend made us believe that she was the one who was crazy and was playing the victim role.

One scenario that I remember where he manipulated my friend will make you feel frustrated as well. So, Angel had excitedly planned a weekend getaway with her dear Ryan, only to have her hopes dashed faster than a porcupine convention. They both worked in a corporate company and had been busy with work. Angel was really looking forward to some quality time together. When the day of their trip approached, Ryan suddenly announced that he had some important work to finish, so he couldn't go.

Angel was disappointed, but still, she tried to understand the situation and suggested postponing the trip to another weekend when they both could be free. But instead of agreeing with Angel, Ryan became defensive and started accusing her. She always tried to control his schedule and make him feel guilty for prioritizing his work. He also accused her of being too demanding.

Angel felt so confused and hurt, and when she dared to express her disappointment, Ryan flipped the script faster than a Hollywood director and painted himself as the victim in this twisted drama. She was so confused and couldn't understand how a simple conversation could turn into a heated argument.

And just when you start thinking that it couldn't get more absurd, that guy—I just can't believe his audacity—managed to turn their mutual friend over to his side, further isolating poor Angel just when she needed support the most. It was just one of many instances where Ryan twisted the truth and made himself look like a victim. I can't imagine the pain Angel went through!

Research has also shown that gaslighting seriously impacts the victim's mental health. A study conducted in 2023 suggested that gaslighting can cause anxiety, depression, and emotional stress in the victim. Moreover, it also revealed that gaslighting can lead to post-traumatic stress symptoms, where victims experience flashbacks, nightmares, and hypervigilance (William et al., 2023).

The Light Seeker Approach - Dealing With Gaslighters Effectively

The "Light Seekers Approach" is your trusty flashlight in the dark alleys of manipulation to dealing with gaslighters. It effectively involves recognizing gaslighting behavior, maintaining a strong sense of self, and asserting boundaries. Awareness is your shield against gaslighting. Here are some of the tips to effectively deal with gaslighters:

- **Understand your worth:** You need to make yourself understand that no one on Earth deserves to be treated this way. You deserve all the kindness and respect possible, so don't tolerate any behavior that ever makes you feel less than you are.
- **Trust your instincts:** If you feel something is off or isn't right, trust your gut and take the step right away

without second-guessing yourself. Is your reality being questioned more often than a plot twist in a soap opera? Back away.

- **Set boundaries:** Set clear boundaries with your partner and let me know what behavior you will or will not tolerate. If the gaslighter starts their act, show them the exit sign.

- **Practice Self-Care**: Taking care of your mental health should always be a priority. Never allow anyone to make you doubt your own thoughts and emotions. Recharge with activities that light you up.

- **Keep a Record**: Document instances of gaslighting behavior. This could be writing down conversations or keeping emails and texts. This record helps you validate your experiences and can be useful if you need to explain the situation to a third party. Think of it as gathering evidence for the grand jury of your sanity.

- **Plan for Safety**: In situations where gaslighting is part of broader abusive behavior, it's crucial to prioritize your safety. This might mean planning a safe way to leave the environment or relationship.

As we explore the Light Seekers Approach, remember that it's not just about protecting yourself, it's about reclaiming your power from those trying to take it away from you. By turning the tables on gaslighting you can handle your manipulators with the light shining in your direction.

Interactive Quiz II: Are You Being

Gaslit?

1. Have you ever doubted your own thoughts in your relationship?

    1. Yes

    2. No

2. Have you ever found yourself second-guessing your own judgment?

    1. Yes

    2. No

3. Have you ever felt like you're constantly walking on eggshells around your partner, afraid of upsetting them?

    1. Yes

    2. No

4. Do you find yourself apologizing for your partner's behavior, even when you know it's not justified?

    1. Yes

    2. No

5. Have you ever felt isolated or cut off from friends and family just because your partner tells you that they are coming between you both?

    1. Yes

    2. No

6. Does your partner ever make you feel like you're

overreacting or being too sensitive?

1. Yes

2. No

7. Does your partner blame you for the problems in the relationship, even when you know you're not at fault?

1. Yes

2. No

8. Do you often feel emotionally drained, anxious, and nervous because of your relationship?

1. Yes

2. No

A higher response of "Yes" may indicate the likelihood that you're experiencing gaslighting.

Chapter 9:

Overcoming the Trap of Breadcrumb Trails

Dating today: where 'breadcrumbing' is common, and carbs are still the enemy. - Unknown

Imagine being lost in a mysterious forest with nothing but towering trees and eerie shadows surrounding you. You're Hansel and Gretel, abandoned, left to fend for themselves. But amidst the fear and uncertainty, they come up with a brilliant plan: leaving a trail of breadcrumbs behind them as they venture deeper into the unknown. With each step they take, the forest seems to grow thicker, the shadows darker, and the silence more deafening. But those breadcrumbs, like tiny beacons of hope, guide them forward, promising safety and salvation at the end of their journey. As they follow the trail, their hearts pound with excitement and trepidation. Every rustle of leaves and snap of twigs sends shivers down their spines, but they press on, driven by the desperate need to find their way home.

Much like Hansel and Gretel, the vast forest of digital dating involves a maze of profiles and conversations that can often feel like being lost in that dark, mysterious forest where the sting of abandonment accompanies this modern-day wilderness. Breadcrumbing is like leaving a trail of digital breadcrumbs to keep someone interested, stringing them along with intermittent messages or attention without real intention of commitment or genuine connection. These digital morsels can seem like beacons of hope in the vast landscape of online dating, promising a potential connection or romance at the end of the journey. But just like the siblings' breadcrumbs, they can also lead to frustration, confusion, and ultimately, a dead end. As we follow these breadcrumbs, our hearts may race with excitement, hoping for a meaningful connection to emerge. So, the modern-day version of "breadcrumbing" can be simply explained as "the act of sending out flirtatious, but non-committal text messages in order to lure a sexual/romantic partner without expending much effort" ("Urban Dictionary: Breadcrumbing.," n.d.).

In more recent years, the concept of breadcrumbing has become increasingly common, especially because of the digital dating era (Power, 2024). People nowadays have more options and chances of indulging in toxic behaviors like ghosting and breadcrumbing because, I mean, who doesn't love a good emotional whiplash, right? In this chapter, we will talk more about just how serious the effects of breadcrumbing are and how to skillfully avoid them.

Breaking Down Breadcrumbing

Have you ever tried to follow a path only to realize that the breadcrumbs you were following have been scattered by birds, leaving you lost? That's what breadcrumbing in the digital world feels like, a tantalizing trail leading nowhere. It's a practice where someone leads you on by dropping 'breadcrumbs' of interest — flirty texts, social media interactions, or occasional dates, but never commits to anything serious. One way breadcrumbing plays out is through inconsistent communication. You receive a flirty text or an engaging message, and just when you start to feel connected, they go silent for days or even weeks.

Then out of the blue, they reappear with another breadcrumb, restarting the cycle.

This inconsistent behavior can leave you feeling confused and emotionally drained. Another manifestation of breadcrumbing is the vague commitment. The breadcrumber might make plans with you but cancel at the last minute, or they may imply a future together but never follow through. For example, they might suggest going on a vacation together or meeting their friends but always find an excuse to postpone it.

Breadcrumbing often occurs on social media platforms. The breadcrumber may like your posts, watch your stories, or leave comments, giving you a sense of connection. However, these interactions are often superficial, lacking any real depth or commitment. While breadcrumbing might seem harmless at first glance, it can lead to emotional distress and feelings of insecurity. Remember, darling, you deserve more than breadcrumbs – you deserve a full loaf of respect, commitment, and genuine connection.

Breadcrumbing is a pervasive part of modern dating culture, a byproduct of the digital age. Recognizing it, understanding its impact, and learning how to navigate it can empower us to build healthier and more fulfilling relationships.

Remember, in the grand maze of dating, you're the one who should be holding the map, not merely following breadcrumbs.

- Five out of nine participants (56%) believe that the

perpetrator engages in breadcrumbing behavior to seek attention from their partners (Khattar et al., 2023).

- Five out of nine (56%) of breadcrumbers want to appear cool in front of their friends or their social groups, which motivates them to engage in such behaviors (Khattar et al., 2023).

- Three out of nine (33%) describe a fear of being alone, whereas 22% of them say they feel insecure and that they are not valued by their peers (Khattar et al., 2023).

- Low self-esteem can truly lead someone to do anything possible just to feel like they are being validated. When someone shows interest in them, they feel better and continue such behavior even though they don't really have any feelings (Lmft, 2024).

- Loneliness can also make you do things like this. A breadcrumber might enjoy closeness and find comfort in it temporarily but that doesn't mean they like you—they are just using you (Lmft, 2024).

- Commitment issues are the most common in today's time where people don't want to put in any effort, but they sure do like to get that effort out of others. They will not offer you anything, but you will find yourself giving them your all (Lmft, 2024).

Before you tackle a problem, it is crucial to understand the details of that problem. Only then can you actually find a solution. The same can be said for dealing with breadcrumbers. Before you learn how to deal with them, you need to understand why they do the things they do. So, here is a list of reasons why people end up being breadcrumbers rather than genuine people who want a serious relationship (Lmft, 2024):

- **Avoidant attachment style:** These people are a bit complicated. They sometimes do want to find a genuine relationship but the second someone gets close to them, they withdraw. Why? Simply because it's out of their comfort zone. Or maybe they just enjoy banging doors in your face, you never know.

- **Narcissistic personality disorder:** Now, this sounds as serious as it is. People who breadcrumb might be narcissistic and it shows when they try to emotionally manipulate you or breadcrumb you simply to deal with their own insecurities.

- **Relationship trauma:** *"I don't think I want to get into anything serious. My ex left me with quite a lot of trust issues and trauma, and I am not ready for a relationship again."* I am sure you have heard something along the lines of this before. And often, you will find that it is people like this who end up hurting you simply because they feel more comfortable being the one causing pain in order to break the pattern that they were used to. This is mostly done in response to interpersonal conflict and as a way of self-preservation.

How to Determine if You Are Being Breadcrumbed

Breadcrumbers will give you attention in the beginning, right? You get what you want. They seem interested and you might go out. Then they start pulling back. They become hot and cold. Sometimes they're interested, sometimes they're not. And you become addicted to that Partial Reward Schedule. You think, *"well this time when I press send, will they text me back, or not?"* And it feels exciting. And so, with securely attached partners their interest in you, and their love for you is continuous. People get so addicted and trapped in this cycle because our brains develop in a way that when we don't know if we will get what we want, it's thrilling. This phenomenon does not align with a healthy relationship and will usually fail. Sometimes, we don't even realize how obvious the signs of a toxic partner are until we have left them. So, here are a few of the signs that you should keep in mind (Lmft, 2024):

- The relationship never really leads to anything. No matter how romantic or flirtatious the person is, your relationship isn't moving toward something. They show little signs of flirting, but they don't follow through. They'll slide into your DMs with a little flame but the minute you say, *"Well hey, I'd love to see you,"* they leave you on 'read' and become *'sooo busy.'*

- The person never makes any plans or even bothers to follow through if you make them. They show interest in a plan, but they don't actually commit. They say things like, *"Yeah, let me know"* or *"Sure, I'll let you know"* or *"Maybe soon we'll see."* They keep you as an option, especially if you're the one who is running after them to make plans.

- Communication is weak and they don't really seem like they care much about what you are saying. They are wildly inconsistent with their communication. One day they might be DMing or texting you all day, and then you don't hear from them for weeks.

- They are always busy and only talk to you when they feel like it. They lack accountability or ownership when you want to talk. So, when you say, *"Every time we try to communicate, you deflect or use humor to change the subject,"* they don't want to engage because they are unavailable.

- They tend to disappear often.

- They like to keep their options open so if you back off, here comes another breadcrumb to keep you on the back burner. They show more interest as soon as you start to back off (Pattemore, 2022).

At the end of the day, your needs are not being met consistently so instead of accepting crumbs, demand the whole tasty loaf. Walk away from somebody who is not able to step up and satisfy your needs. Their effort will show you the position they want in your life. Not their words in their texts, not their fire emojis, not their promises or intentions – their effort!

Tools to Cope with and Move Beyond Breadcrumbs Relationships

Being in a relationship with a breadcrumber can be emotionally draining, and it can leave you with zero motivation to do anything else. Oftentimes, when you find yourself with a breadcrumber, they will use manipulative tactics like ghosting and gaslighting. In these scenarios, people often become vulnerable and take the blame on themselves and that is the first step toward losing yourself.

It is important that once you have left the person who had been feeding off of you, you take some time to cope and move beyond what happened. I mean, don't you think you need some time to recover after coming out of a game that feels like a Sudoku in which the numbers just don't add up? In cases like this, you need to focus on yourself.

There is no one more important than your own self, and that is all you should focus on. Here are a few things that you should try in times like these:

- Surround yourself with people who love and support you. After the traumatic experience of being with someone who has you questioning your own worth, it is important to be around people who remind you just how amazing you are.

- Give therapy a shot. Believe it or not, therapy has been highly effective in cases like this and is definitely worth a try.

- Work on setting your boundaries. Now that you have experienced the worst, you need to make sure that you never have to go through that again. Think about what you do and don't accept in a relationship anymore, even if it's something as silly as a "no snoring" rule. Hey! We all have our own unique dealbreakers.

- Go no-contact. I mean, what do you do when you find

that something is making you sick? You make sure you stay away from it, right? So, make sure that that person can never come back into your life.

How to React When You're Being Breadcrumbed

Silence can sometimes be a good thing but there are times when it's important to speak out. Once you have understood the signs and gathered that you are being breadcrumbed, the next step is to do something about it, and trust me when I say there is plenty that you can do.

- Call them out on their behavior and tell them that it is no longer acceptable. Being direct is your best option.

- Set boundaries and let them know that things can no longer be the same.

- Point out the fact that the two of you are not on the same page and that this is not acceptable to you.

- Decide if you want to continue the relationship, and if you don't, it is best to let them know that you don't want to associate with them anymore.

Regaining Self-Worth After a String of

Shallow Interactions

Individuals who experienced breadcrumbing reported higher levels of stress, anxiety and depression. It creates a form of emotional manipulation that creates an ambiguous state in the relationship which contributes to these adverse psychological outcomes. This can lead to feelings of rejection, and low self-esteem and even trigger symptoms similar to post-traumatic stress disorder (PTSD). One of the most important things to remember is that it's not your loss if you distance yourself. In fact, it is a good thing that you are no longer with a person who made you question your own self-worth. Every time you look in the mirror, remind yourself that you deserve better than this. Most people let others' words impact them and question their self-worth, and if you find yourself in a similar situation, then you need to work on regaining your confidence because you, my dear, are the showstopper of the show.

And that is all you need. Love yourself the way you deserve to be loved before you find someone else to do it for you because no one can love you properly until you do it first.

The only way to resist a breadcrumber is if you have enough self-esteem and confidence to the point where you know what you deserve and no one can change that (Hope Therapy & Counselling Services, 2023).

Wrap Up

Well, well, well, look at you! You now have a detailed idea of not only what breadcrumbing is but also how to identify and deal with it. Now, just to embed all of this in your mind, let's have a recap, shall we?

- Inconsistent behavior, weak communication, and no effort are all signs of breadcrumbing.

- People breadcrumb for different reasons including attention, loneliness, and narcissism.

- Breadcrumbing can have an impact on you and make you question your self-worth. Breadcrumbers can make you emotionally disturbed and give you trust issues.

- It is important to stand up for yourself and call out the other person. Remind them that this isn't how you deserve to be treated.

- Focus on yourself and let go of someone who doesn't give you what you need.

The next time you find yourself being breadcrumbed, remember that there are plenty of fish in the sea and that you have the rest of your life to enjoy. It is much better to be single and love yourself than be with someone who makes you question your own mind. There is no better version of you than the one you love and protect.

Chapter 10:

Effective Communication in Digital Romance

Between what is said and not meant, and what is meant and not said, most love is lost. – Kahlil Gibran

Have you ever felt like you were hitting it off with someone on Tinder, only to have a simple misunderstanding in a text message to push you apart? Maybe you've felt so confused or frustrated by a person's messages that their whole approach just didn't make any sense to you anymore. If so, you're not alone!

We all know that good communication is like the glue that holds any modern-day relationship together, even when you're talking through screens. In the world of digital dating, a misplaced emoji or a misinterpreted message can sometimes end a promising connection. To navigate the twists and turns of modern love, it's essential to master the art of communication in today's world.

So, this chapter is going to serve as the ultimate crash course in the art of digital dating communication. We'll be diving straight into the wild world of online interaction, where decoding text messages is like cracking the Da Vinci code, and expressing emotions through screens is as tricky as tackling a Rubik's Cube.

But worry not, my friend, for I have a treasure trove of tips and tricks to help you navigate this digital dating world with grace and confidence. By the time you reach the end of this chapter, you'll have enough knowledge to tackle everything from virtual flirtation to setting boundaries in a world with seemingly none.

So, let's explore the standards of healthy relationships in the digital age. Now is the time to swipe right on communication mastery and swipe left on awkward online encounters.

Healthy Relationship Standards in a Digital Age

In the digital age, building and maintaining a healthy relationship requires more effort and adaptability. Here are some of the essential elements of a healthy relationship:

Effective communication

Communication is the magical potion that fuels the flame of every successful relationship. In the digital age, where emojis are used to express feelings and virtual chats have become the norm, it's more crucial than ever before to master the art of open and clear communication. Active listening, authenticity, and empathy are consistent steps toward relationship bliss.

And here's the kicker: in the theater of communication, it's a duet, not a solo act! So, both partners need to be honest and open with each other. After all, it is the joint effort of both sides that keeps the relationship boat sailing smoothly even through the stormy sea of digital love (Aislin et al., 2022).

Trust and transparency

Trust is the backbone of every healthy relationship, but when it comes to online dating, it becomes hard to trust anyone. You don't even know if the person behind the screen is real or not. Don't trust anyone blindly. You have to carefully analyze the other person before putting your complete trust in them. Try to be clear about your intentions, expectations, and boundaries, and make sure you maintain a balance between sharing personal information and respecting each other's privacy.

Emotional support and empathy

In the digital age, where we can easily connect with others, we sometimes forget that behind every online persona, there's a human just like you with emotions, vulnerabilities, and needs. They also need emotional support, just like you do. So, it's important to show genuine interest in their life, offer a listening ear, and make sure you validate their feelings. Try to understand each other by putting yourself in one another's shoes. When you validate their emotions and feelings, they reciprocate this as well.

Quality time and boundaries

Craving quality time tells you that you're in a healthy relationship. To strengthen your bond with your partner, you need to dedicate your uninterrupted moments. In the age of social media and networking, it's hard to just stay on one screen. On one side, you're chatting with your partner, and on the other, you're scrolling Instagram side by side. It's like you scratch your head and rub your belly at the same time—tricky, but oh-so exhilarating!

But beware, for those replies can speak volumes that can leave your partner wondering if they're not enough! So, you need to make an effort to show them that you're genuinely interested. Try to opt for calls over text messages. Set a specific time to focus solely on each other, allowing for deeper connections and uninterrupted conversation.

Resolving conflict and compromising

No relationship is perfect or devoid of conflicts, but the way you address and resolve them tells you the strength of your bond. In the digital age, misunderstanding can easily arise due to a lack of nonverbal cues. Whenever a conflict occurs, take your time to reflect and communicate calmly.

Note it down, if you need to. Write, "Don't fight over text messages," as fighting over them will only make things worse. Call your partner or meet up with them in person, if possible. From there, find mutually agreeable solutions. Remember, relationships require effort, and if you're not ready to make an effort, then don't be in one.

Research has shown that digital communication has enhanced relationships in one way and strained them in another. On the one hand, it allows new ways to show affection and support. For example, platforms like Instagram and Snapchat provide you with opportunities for sharing moments and expressing intimacy. On the other hand, excessive use of it can lead to misunderstanding, jealousy, and conflict (Lenhart et al., 2015). So, it's important to set boundaries and maintain balance in digital communication to ensure your relationship is healthy.

Establish Clear Communication Norms

In digital dating, where misunderstandings can easily arise, it's important to establish communication norms. Try to do the following:

- **Avoid misinterpretation:** Communication over text messages lacks tone, facial expressions, and body language, leading to misinterpretation. Clear communication norms help you to convey your intentions and emotions accurately and reduce the risk of misunderstanding in your relationship.

- **Set expectations:** Clear and transparent communication helps you build trust by demonstrating reliability, honesty, and accountability in your relationship.

- **Resolve conflicts or disagreements:** Clear communication norms can help you address issues openly, express your concerns constructively, and work toward resolving them together.

Tips for Establishing Clear Communication Norms in Online Dating

Here are some practical tips for establishing clear communication norms in online dating:

- **Be open about your expectations:** When it comes to online dating, every individual has different expectations. Communicate your intentions and expectations at the start of the relationship to help foster a more compatible and respectful connection. Let your partner know whether you're looking for a long-term relationship or not. This will help you and the other person decide whether you can continue or not.

- **Use clear and concise language:** It is important to use clear and straightforward language in your communication to avoid any kind of misunderstanding. Try to be specific when expressing your feelings, thoughts, and preferences to ensure mutual understanding.

- **Listen actively:** Make sure that you listen to your partner's concerns and preferences actively. Make them feel that you genuinely care, pay attention to their style, and be responsive and empathetic in your responses.

You have to be careful when you're setting communication norms in your relationship, especially when you're dating online, otherwise, it can ruin your relationship. I know people who initially started off their relationship without giving much thought to communication but later realized that they had different expectations and the relationship ended up fizzling out.

Setting Boundaries in Virtual Interactions

Boundaries are those unsung heroes that keep every relationship healthy. Just like an invisible force of the interpersonal universe, boundaries are the secret sauce that keeps misunderstandings and conflicts away. These boundaries guide behaviors and ensure that both sides feel respected, valued, and safe within the sacred confines of the relationship. Without these boundaries, there will be misunderstandings and disagreements.

So, note these words of wisdom: At the very beginning of your relationship journey, lay down those boundary bricks with care and consideration. I'm not telling you to build walls but rather to create a blueprint for mutual respect and understanding that will stand the test of time.

How to Effectively Set Boundaries in Virtual Interactions

Here's how you can set boundaries in virtual interaction effectively:

- It's important to respect each other's schedule and personal space. Discuss with your partner the time you both think will be convenient and suitable to chat or call. Consider each other's working hours, commitments, time zones, and preferences for morning or evening. Discussing it beforehand can avoid the misunderstanding that the other person is ignoring you.

- Decide what kind of information you're comfortable sharing in your online interactions. Discuss topics like sharing photos or discussing sensitive or private matters. Respect each other's boundaries and don't force anyone to share what they don't want to share.

Research has shown that people navigate privacy based on several factors such as their sense of control and awareness, social norms, and trust in the platform provider (Stutzman & Hartzog, 2009). For example, when it comes to sharing photos, people prefer sharing on Snapchat as the other person can't save it, and even if they do, the photo owner will get to know that the other person took a screenshot (Cyr et al., 2014).

Key Takeaways

Here are the key takeaways from this chapter:

- Healthy relationship standards include effective communication, providing emotional support, building trust, and respecting each other's boundaries.

- Setting clear communication norms and clearing boundaries are important components of fostering healthy connections.

If you're struggling in your relationship and end up fighting regularly due to misunderstanding, try to use the tips we've discussed above!

Chapter 11:

Achieving Proficiency at the Art of Textual Conversation

Texting is a brilliant way to miscommunicate how you feel, and misinterpret what other people mean. - Unknown

Just like a well-prepared meal, a good textual conversation needs the right ingredients. It needs a pinch of humor, a dash of wit, a spoonful of empathy, and a ladle full of sincerity. In our digital age, text-based communication has become the primary mode of interaction for many. It's used in daily life and online dating.

We've all been there: the phone buzzes, you glance down, and there it is – a text message from that special someone. The simple act of texting plays a significant role in how we form and maintain romantic relationships today. For instance, frequent and prompt responses indicate interest and availability.

Texting is often our initial contact with potential partners. Remember the last time you exchanged numbers with someone you met online or at a social event? Chances are that your first communication wasn't a phone call but a text message or DM. The initial exchange sets the tone for the relationship. A witty, well-crafted message can spark interest and excitement, while poorly timed or thoughtless text can lead to disappointment.

Becoming better at the art of textual conversation is akin to learning a new language – one that is essential for navigating our digital landscape. It's more than just an exchange of words – this involves establishing connections, expressing emotions, and building relationships.

So next time you pick up your phone to send a text, remember you're not just typing words but weaving together a blend of human connections.

Texting is an art that helps convey emotions and intentions accurately. For example, using emojis, GIFs, and memes can help express feelings that words alone might not capture. They serve as the digital equivalent of facial expressions and body language, adding depth to the conversation.

Effective texting can help maintain long-distance relationships. The act of texting can bridge physical distance and foster emotional closeness.

Let's begin by highlighting the importance of textual conversation in today's digital dating era!

The Importance of Text Conversation in Modern Dating

On the stage of modern dating, texting takes a central place alongside the classic acts of in-person conversation and phone calls. In the whirlwind romance of digital dating, texting serves as a silent messenger that bridges the gap between two potential lovebirds. Whether it's a flirty compliment or a heartfelt confession, texting sets the stage for the spark to fly and for bonds to deepen. It's a small window into your love interests' personality, giving you a taste of their humor, intellect, and emotional depth, but why exactly is texting so important in the modern dating arena, you may wonder? Well, let's count the ways:

- **It keeps you in contact throughout the day:** When it comes to online dating, texting allows for ongoing communication throughout the day. Though phone calls seem better than texting, it's practically impossible to stay on a call all day long, so those little messages throughout the day can make you feel more connected to your partner. Texting provides a constant connection with our partners. This constant connectivity can foster a sense of closeness and familiarity.

- **It serves as a platform for conflict resolution:** In today's world, texting can be a place where conflicts are solved and, unfortunately, initiate. Disagreements can arise from misinterpreted messages or unmet expectations around response times. However, when used thoughtfully, texting can also be an effective medium for resolving disputes. Apologizing via text gives the other person time to process your words without feeling pressure to respond immediately.

- **It's a great way to make each other happy:** These digital love notes can brighten up mundane routines. A cute little morning text, an affectionate message in the middle of the day, or a goodnight text from your partner can bring a smile to your face making you feel cherished. It's akin to finding a surprise note in your lunch box – unexpected yet delightful.

- **It keeps long-distance relationships alive:** Effective texting can help maintain long-distance relationships. The act of texting can bridge physical distance and foster emotional closeness. You might not feel connected to people unless you are texting, and when you feel connected, interest develops and that's how most relationships build love and connection.

- **It acts as a medium of expression:** Text messages can act as a medium to express feelings that might be difficult to convey in person. You may find yourself pouring your heart out in a late-night conversation via text, revealing aspects of yourself that you might not have in a face-to-face chat. This exchange can build intimacy and foster trust between two people, making it an essential aspect of digital dating.

Interestingly, research suggests that waiting for a text message from a loved one can trigger the release of dopamine, the "feel-good" hormone, in our brain. This neurochemical effect explains why we often feel a rush of happiness when our phones buzz with a message from that special someone.

The magic of text messages lies in their content, in the anticipation they create, and the emotions they evoke. They've transformed the way we connect, making even the simplest of interactions a source of joy and excitement. From that vibrating phone on your desk to the glowing screen under your pillow at night, text messages from a love interest have become the modern-day love letters that keep our hearts fluttering.

Text conversations have not only become a central component of modern dating but have also reshaped the way people connect in romantic relationships. A study in 2013 analyzing the role of texting in relationships found that texting behavior differs between genders, as women are more likely to use texting as a way to avoid face-to-face interaction, while men on the other hand use texting for distraction (Schade et al., 2013).

Remember, like any tool, the impact of texting depends on how well we use it. An improperly used compass can lead you off course, just as thoughtless texting can derail a budding relationship. To avoid misunderstandings, let's discuss some strategies.

Expressing Emotions and Intentions Through Texts

It's essential to be mindful of our digital communication, as it forms the foundation of many modern love stories. Texting offers a unique platform for connecting, but sometimes it becomes challenging to make the other person understand your emotions and intentions. So, here are some simple strategies that you can use to express your emotions through text without being misunderstood:

Strategies for Effectively Expressing Yourself Over Text

- **Choose your words thoughtfully:** You have to be very careful with your words and tone as per the situation to ensure your sincerity. For example, instead of saying, "*I guess we could hang out if you want,*" try something like, *"I'd love to spend time with you if you're up for it."*

- **Utilize emojis and emoticons:** Emojis can help you convey emotions that words alone may not capture. They add nuance to a simple text message. For example, instead of a simple "take care" text, add a heart emoji at the end to show your genuine emotion.

- **Be mindful of timing:** Timing is very crucial when it comes to texting. Avoid sensitive discussions late at night or during your busy hours. Just send a simple text like, *"Hey honey, I know this is important to you, and I don't want to mess it up over text. Is it fine if I call you in the morning?"*

- **Ask for clarification:** If you're unsure about the tone or meaning of your partner's text, don't hesitate to ask them again to avoid misunderstanding. For example, you can say, *"I'm not sure I understand what you mean. Lost in text. Could you clarify?"*

If you're not good at texting, don't worry—you'll learn over time. Some text as if others can read their mind. But with time and practice, the importance of words and comprehension becomes second nature. You'll be texting 'brb' (be right back), 'ttyl' (talk to you later) or 'omg (oh my god) in no time. It makes communication swift, efficient, and makes for a stronger bond.

Keeping the Conversation Engaging

Just like the anticipation of opening a beautifully wrapped gift, the excitement of receiving a text message from someone you're interested in is a unique thrill. It's this modern-day version of waiting for a handwritten letter to arrive; only now it comes with a specific ringtone and pops up on a screen. In order to maintain an interesting conversation over text, you need to learn a mix of engagement strategies. Here are some tips:

- **Ask open-ended questions:** Instead of asking questions that elicit a simple "yes" or "no" response, ask questions that encourage detailed answers. For example, instead of *"Did you have a nice day?"*, ask, *"How did you spend your day?"*

- **Share personal stories:** If you're at a reasonable level in your relationship, and comfortable sharing personal stories, then do it often, as this can deepen the connection between you and your partner.

- **Use humor:** Humor is a great way to keep your conversation engaging. Share jokes, memes, and funny observations with your partner. Just be mindful of their sense of humor and avoid making sensitive and dark jokes.

- **Be yourself:** Authenticity is the key to maintaining engagement in your conversation. Don't be afraid to express your true emotions and thoughts, even if they differ from norms. People are more likely to connect with those they find genuine and sincere.

Each of these elements plays a critical role in our online interactions. They help us overcome the limitations of text-based communication, allowing us to express our feelings and intentions more effectively.

How to Keep Them Wanting More Through Texting

Think about your favorite book. The gripping plot, the complex characters, and the unexpected twists keep you turning page after page into the night. Just like a good book that you can't put down, captivating messages have the power to grip your attention and keep you glued to your phone screen, eagerly awaiting the next notification. Now, imagine if you could create that same level of anticipation and excitement through your text messages.

A well-crafted text message can spark curiosity, convey interest, and establish a deep connection, all without saying a word in person.

Firstly, timing is everything in texting. Just like a well-timed joke can elicit laughter, a thoughtfully timed text can create anticipation and excitement. Knowing when to send what message can make all the difference. For example, if you know your potential partner is a morning person, sending an upbeat good morning text can start their day off on a positive note and keep you in their thoughts throughout the day.

Secondly, the content of your texts is vital. In the digital world, words are your primary mode of expression.

Hence, they need to be chosen carefully.

A good text message is like a tasty hors d'oeuvre – it should satisfy but leave them craving more.

Lastly, remember the importance of balance. Just like in a dance, both partners need to contribute equally for it to flow smoothly. If one person is always initiating the conversation or carrying it forward, it might lead to an imbalance and eventual communication breakdown or it can lead to one of the digital dating dilemmas, like ghosting.

In the end, effective texting is an art form that needs practice and patience. It revolves around creating an engaging narrative that keeps your potential partner interested and invested. Maintaining intrigue ensures they are always looking forward to your texts.

. Here are 10 texts to keep them captivated, wanting more, and a bit cheeky:

- **I had a vivid dream about you last night...**

- **The thing that makes me smile the most about you is...**

- **Make sure you put me on your 'to-do list today...**

- **I have a secret that I can only tell you in person...**

- **I can't decide what I want more, food or you. Food...No, you. Maybe, food on you on our next date...**

- **Your body is 65% water and guess what? I'm very thirsty at the moment...**

- Do you wanna know the first two things that come to mind when I think of you?...

- Do you have any idea what it is about you that turns me on the most?...

- What 3 wishes would you ask the genie if I were a magical lamp and you rubbed me?...

- Hey, stop thinking about me. I need to focus...

Wrap Up

Becoming better at the art of texting can be a game-changer in your personal life. Don't focus on sending messages, but on creating experiences that leave the recipient wanting more. So, choose your words wisely, add a dash of intrigue, and watch as your relationships flourish. Try to make sure that:

- Instead of revealing everything in one go, try to leave certain things open-ended or hinted at, and then watch the magic happen. This will not only increase their curiosity but also leave them wanting to know more.

- Plant seeds for future interaction during texting such as by teasing your partner about upcoming events or hinting at something exciting that you want to show them or tell them about. This can leave your partner looking forward to the next interaction.

- Instead of responding immediately to every text,

occasionally space out your responses to build anticipation and make them more curious. This doesn't mean that you intentionally start ignoring their messages and playing games, but rather you allow a little time between responses to heighten the anticipation of what you'll say next.

A note about Sexting

Just like driving on a foggy night, sexting and sending photos over the internet can be a treacherous journey. The road ahead is unclear, and what seemed like a harmless action could lead to unforeseen accidents. Every time you send a photo or a sensitive message, you're entrusting your personal information to not just the recipient, but the platform you're using. This might not seem relevant if you're only sending images to someone you trust, but what happens if they decide to share those images without your permission? The potential repercussions are far-reaching and can include job loss, public humiliation, and sometimes legal consequences. Not to mention, there's an emotional toll. While it might feel exciting and intimate at the moment, the aftermath of sexting can bring about feelings of vulnerability, regret, and anxiety – especially if the relationship ends badly. Remember these photos are digitized which lasts a lifetime. Unfortunately, we can't trust another person through screens.

Texting is a master skill in online dating. It not only helps build relationships but can aid you in making a healthy one. And just like a good book, this involves leaving them eagerly awaiting the next chapter.

Chapter 12:

Decoding Emojis, GIFs, and Memes in Modern Romance Language

Texting is an art, but decoding texts is a science. - Unknown

Imagine you and your partner have a plan to meet up later in the evening, but you unexpectedly got caught up in a last-minute commitment, so you hurriedly reach for your cell phone to send them a message:

"Hey, I'm so sorry. I won't be able to make it tonight."

And you get a simple response: *"Fine."* And now you're not sure if that was just a neutral acknowledgment or a passive-aggressive response, am I right? You feel overwhelmed with a mix of guilt and disappointment because their reply has left you feeling misunderstood and unvalued. Maybe they don't mean to devalue you, though—maybe it's just the way they said it because a simple text like "Fine" could easily be misinterpreted.

Now imagine, instead of just *"fine,"* they add a sad emoji ☐ in it. It now feels different, doesn't it? It softens the tone and conveys a sense of understanding, making the text appear less harsh and more empathetic.

Do you see how a simple emoji can make such a big difference? In today's digital dating world, where words alone often struggle to capture true emotions, emojis, GIFs, and memes have stepped up to fill the gap. They make you laugh, blush, or may even turn you on sometimes. Yes, you read that right! They actually do. According to research at Edge Hill University, those who use emojis in their text messages tend to have more active sex lives (Kaye & Schweiger, 2023).

But how did we come to rely so much on these emojis, GIFs, and memes to express ourselves in matters of the heart? How did modern romance languages evolve over time? In this chapter, we'll unravel the mysteries of modern dating language. We'll explore the rich history and cultural significance of emojis and GIFs, and we'll also discuss the meanings behind our favorite symbols. Along the way, I'll provide you with some practical tips for using them effectively in conversations.

So, let's begin with their historical evolution!

The History and Evolution of Emojis, GIFs, and Memes

A picture is worth a thousand words. As archaic as this saying may seem, it holds true in the digital landscape where emojis, GIFs, and text abbreviations have become the norm for expressing emotions and intentions. The history of emojis, GIFs, and memes is fascinating. It all started with simple emoticons such as a classic smiley face :-) or a winking face ;-). People relied on these emoticons to infuse their texts with emotions. However, as technology has advanced and communication platforms have begun diversifying, the need for more expressive forms of visual communication has also increased, and as a result, we have entered the world of emojis, GIFs, and memes.

Emojis

Emojis are modern-day descendants of emoticons. Consider how emojis have revolutionized digital communication. These small digital images or icons express emotions or represent ideas in concise, visually engaging ways. For instance, it's easier to send a heart emoji than to spell out *"I love you."* It saves time and adds a playful element to the conversation. These small and colorful symbols offer a wide range of symbols to express everything from joy ☐ to disappointment ☐, and from sadness ☐ to frustration ☐. With every passing year, emojis have grown more sophisticated and have started to include diverse skin tones, gender representation, and even cultural symbols.

GIFs

Let's look at GIFs. Short for Graphics Interchange Format, these are essentially animated images that can convey complex emotions or reactions better than words can. For example, sending a GIF of a character laughing hysterically can be more impactful than simply typing "lol." GIFs have also emerged as a dynamic way of expressing emotions and conveying reactions. They have evolved from basic animations to a rich tapestry of moving images sourced from movies, TV shows, and pop culture moments. Whether it's a clip of a dramatic eye roll or someone dancing with joy, GIFs add flavor and humor to your online conversations.

Memes

Memes have become a new language in today's world. They represent a unique fusion of humor, social commentary, and internet culture. From the iconic "LOLcats" of the 2000s internet to the viral "distracted boyfriend" meme of today, memes have kept us laughing.

The kind of influence these emojis, GIFs, and memes have on us is unbelievable. A study by Instagram revealed that more than 50% of all captions and comments on the platform contain at least one emoji (Instagram Emoji Study, 2016).

Understanding Emojis

Emojis play a very essential role when it comes to online dating. Different emojis can have different meanings. Let's find out the meaning behind common emojis used in dating language:

- **Heart eye emoji** □: This emoji signifies admiration, infatuation, or romantic interest. If someone sends you this emoji, it means they find you attractive and charming.

- **Heart eye cat emoji** ☐: This emoji is similar to a heart eye emoji and is used to express admiration and love with a cute twist. When someone finds you adorable, cute, and irresistible, they send you this emoji.

- **Kissy face emoji** ☐: This emoji is used to convey the desire to kiss sometimes or to express the feeling of love and romance. It expresses affection in a playful and flirtatious manner.

- **Blushing face emoji** ☐: This emoji is usually used to convey shyness or a blush in response to a compliment or flirtation.

- **Heart emoji** ❤☐: A red heart emoji is a classic symbol of deep love, passion, and affection, and is commonly used to express romantic feelings or to show fondness for someone.

Different colors of heart emoji represent different meanings. For example, the red heart represents passionate and deep love, the pink heart suggests sweetness and affection, and the yellow heart symbolizes friendship and warmth. A blue heart, on the other hand, represents loyalty, trust, or a sense of peace.

Decoding GIFs

A GIF serves as a unique means of communication that allows people to convey reactions or feelings in a way that words alone may struggle to capture. The animated nature of GIFs allows them to add depth and nuance to our online conversations and makes it easier for us to express emotions in our relationships.

Popular GIFs in the Digital Dating World

Here are some popular GIFs you can use in conversation with your date according to the situation:

- **Animated hearts and love symbol GIFs:** GIFs that feature animated hearts and love symbols are used to express love and infatuation.

- **Flirty wink and smile:** GIFs of people smiling and winking in a flirtatious way can playfully convey interest or attraction.

- **Holding hand or hug GIFs:** GIFs that depict romantic gestures such as kisses, hugs, and holding hands are used to express intimacy and affection.

Making Sense of Memes

A meme refers to a humorous image, video, piece of text, or GIF that spreads across the internet, mainly on social media apps, and with slight variation. Memes can be created about anything from current events to pop culture references. The best part about memes is that anyone can create them. Memes have become a unique language unto themselves in digital communication. They aren't limited by linguistic barriers and rely on visual imagery and cultural references to convey complex emotions and messages in a concise and relatable way.

Popular Dating-Related Memes

Here are some popular dating memes:

- **Distracted boyfriend:** This meme features a picture of a man walking with his girlfriend while turning his head to check out another woman passing near them. This meme is often used to depict situations that involve being distracted by something new and interesting.

- **First date vs 100th date:** This meme consists of two images side by side. One picture shows the situation of a couple at an early stage of their relationship and the other shows the stage where the relationship is established. This meme humorously constructs the difference between early stage dating and an established relationship.

Cultural Differences

Interpretations of emojis, GIFs, and memes can significantly vary across cultures. Every culture has different perspectives and norms that impact the meaning of emojis or memes in them. For example, a thumbs-up emoji might be interpreted positively in Western culture but in some Middle Eastern or Asian cultures, it might seem offensive. Similarly, a GIF may be considered funny in one culture but might have a different effect in another due to differences in comedy styles or jokes.

Memes are also highly cultural-specific. A study by Swift Key in 2015 found significant cultural differences in emoji usage (SwiftKey Emoji Report, 2015).

Understanding these cultural variations is crucial for effective communication in online dating across diverse cultures. Misinterpretation of emojis and GIFs can cause misunderstandings and conflicts, especially when two people are from different cultural backgrounds.

The Do's & Don'ts

Though emojis, GIFs, and memes help you in digital communication, some situations require you to stick with words. Used correctly, they can help you establish rapport and express emotions that words alone might fail to convey.

Here are some quick do's and don'ts that you need to consider when it comes to using these symbols:

Do's

- Use emojis when you find it hard to express your emotions. It also helps you to enhance the tone of your text, so if you want to make an intense situation a little lighter, you can use an emoji.

- If you want to lighten up the mood of your partner, you can use GIFs.

- If you and your partner have a similar sense of humor,

sharing memes can enhance the bond between you.

Don't

- Don't overuse them as this can suggest immaturity and insincerity.

- Be cautious of misinterpretation. Choose emojis or GIFs that align with the tone and context of the conversation.

- If your partner seems unresponsive toward your emojis and memes, avoid using them and respect their boundaries.

- Don't send a GIF at the wrong time. Make sure the situation calls for a GIF before sending one.

- Always consider if the content could potentially offend the other person. Steer clear from sharing memes about sensitive issues such as politics or religion unless you're certain about where the person stands on these matters.

Wrap Up

Digital dating requires clear and more careful communication than traditional dating. Emojis, GIFs, and memes can help you express yourself easier when you find it hard to make the other person understand with words. Each of these elements plays a crucial role in our online interactions. They help us overcome the limitations of text-based communication, allowing us to express our feelings and intentions more effectively. The rise of emojis, GIFs, memes, and textspeak has forever transformed the landscape of digital communication. It's reshaped how we relate to each other online and made our online conversations richer and more expressive.

The golden rule here is balance. Your messages should reflect a mix of words, emojis, GIFs, memes, and textspeak to keep the conversation engaging without overwhelming your potential partner. After mastering these digital dating languages, remember that nothing beats genuine connection. Keep conversations real and honest.

As the saying goes, *"Be yourself – everyone else is taken."*

Chapter 13:

Shifting From Surface-Level to Deep Connection

Connection is why we're here; it is what gives purpose and meaning to our lives. – Brene Brown

Just like a tree can't grow tall and strong without deep roots, meaningful relationships can't flourish without deep connection. In the digital age, the quest for love often feels like speed-dating on steroids, with swipes dictating the pace of our romantic lives. It's easy to fall for the fast love phenomenon. Imagine meeting someone new and, within a week, you're already picking out matching outfits for your next date. Let's be real: is this whirlwind romance built on genuine compatibility, or are we just riding the high of a new connection? A true connection goes beyond shared interests or hobbies – this involves mutual understanding, respect, and vulnerability. In the world of online dating and social media, everything is fast paced. Would you really say that your relationship is born out of compatibility or an actual emotional bond?

As we navigate the maze of online dating and instant gratification, it's crucial to pause and consider what truly sustains a relationship. Sure, physical attraction is the spark, but without a deeper connection, the flame can fizzle out faster than a left swipe on a bad profile pic. What happens when the initial excitement wears off? If you're left with nothing but memories of good angles and witty chat-up lines, it's a sign you might be missing a foundational bond. Love, like a poorly made souffle, can deflate just as swiftly as it rises, leaving one to ponder what remains in the dish once the initial heat dissipates. It's in these moments that one must appreciate the base ingredients: respect, admiration, and a deep connection. For its these elements, more than the thrilling rise, that sustain a relationship through the everyday bake of life. True compatibility isn't just about riding the waves of attraction; it's about enjoying the steady boat ride together, even when the waters are calm.

In this chapter, we're going to explore the trials and triumphs of digital dating. We'll dissect the importance of building a connection that's more than just skin deep. At the end of the day, it's the deep, genuine connections that not only survive the test of time but also enrich our lives. So, let's dive right in!

Understanding Genuine Connections

You know when you walk into a crowded room, your eyes naturally seek out familiar faces? That's a bit like online dating. Amid the sea of profiles and attractive photos, we're all searching for that one familiar soul, someone who resonates with us on a deeper level. When we talk about genuine connections, many people confuse chemistry with a true emotional genuine connection. If you think the feeling of butterflies fluttering in your stomach or the flying sparks every time you touch is a genuine bond, then think again. A genuine connection is more than swooning over your partner, it is about finding a partner who can promise you a future filled with happiness tethered by trust, shared interests, and deep understanding. Maybe even a few inside jokes to add to the mix. A genuine connection forms the foundation of any enduring relationship. It encompasses shared interests and life goals, as well as a deep-seated trust that nurtures long-term commitment.

In today's era of catfishing, unearthing genuine connections is a formidable challenge. It's far from simple – certainly no walk in the park – to discover a relationship steeped in authenticity. It seems many have lost sight of what it truly means to be genuine. Here's a little secret to navigating this landscape: authenticity starts with being true to yourself and honest with others. Only then can the foundation of your relationship solidify, paving the way for trust and a deeper bond with your partner. Authenticity isn't just about being honest but rather accepting your flaws and vulnerabilities so that when you have a partner, you can open up to them and embrace these things. Only then can you form a safe space between your partner and yourself (Faster Capital, n.d.).

Deep connections play a vital role in our lives through communication. When we connect deeply with others, we're more open and honest in our communication. This doesn't mean talking about our day or our favorite TV shows, although that can be fun. It means sharing our fears, hopes, dreams, and insecurities. For example, telling a love interest about your anxiety over an upcoming job interview shows vulnerability and fosters a deeper connection.

Also, deep connections enhance our empathy. When we understand someone on a profound level, we can put ourselves in their shoes more easily. This empathy is about more than just feeling sorry for someone – this involves understanding their emotions and motivations. For example, if your partner shares that they are struggling with depression, you're more likely to empathize with their experience and provide emotional support.

Moreover, deep connections contribute to our sense of belonging. Humans are social creatures, and we crave connection. When we connect deeply with others, we feel seen, heard, and valued. This sense of belonging can be as simple as having a partner who understands your quirky sense of humor or as profound as finding someone who loves you unconditionally.

The Challenges of Creating Genuine Connections Online

Online dating is more than a platform to meet potential partners. It's a tool that can help us understand ourselves better. First, it allows us to clarify our wants and deal breakers. Second, online dating encourages self-presentation which can lead to self-discovery. Crafting a profile pushes us to reflect on who we are and how we want to be perceived. Third, it provides an opportunity to develop communication skills. The art of messaging someone you're interested in needs tact, empathy, and authenticity. This involves exploring human connection in its many forms. Genuine connection isn't found easily but is worth the search. It is much like life itself – an experience filled with surprises, disappointments, lessons, and hopefully, meaningful connections. It's a mirror that reflects our wants, fears, strengths, and vulnerabilities. As we swipe left or right, we're not just choosing potential partners. We're also choosing who we want to be.

Digital dating definitely comes with challenges. Yet, these obstacles can teach us resilience and discernment while all of us are out there sharing tales of how useful these dating apps are, what we completely forget is that with new advancements come new problems. With the advancement of dating apps, people have become less likely to form genuine connections with others simply because they can't really know someone completely until they meet them (BetterHelp Editorial Team, 2024).

Despite its hurdles, remember that every grain of sand on the beach is unique, just as every individual in the digital dating world is unique. It might take time and patience to find that special grain. It's a testament to our resilience and adaptability, reflecting our ceaseless quest for connection in an ever-evolving world. Here are some challenges you might face while trying to build a genuine bond with someone online (Faster Capital, n.d.).

Miscommunication

Navigating the digital dating world can be like playing a game of telephone with your Wi-Fi on the fritz – messages get jumbled, intentions are lost in translation, and emojis don't always mean what you think they do. For example, in emoji overload you may send a winky face, intending a bit of flirty charm, but they see it and think you've got something in your eye. And what about punctuation perils? The difference between, *"Let's eat, darling"* and *"Let's eat darling"* can make your date wonder if they're on the menu rather than on your mind. A misplaced comma can change everything in communication. Also, in digital dating, timing is everything. Send a message too soon, and you're overly eager. Reply too late, and you're disinterested. When our memes misfire, we can leave the other person questioning our intent. The meme you send might be all the rage, but it's met with a *"Huh?"* What's hilarious to one can be hieroglyphics to another, proving that sometimes, a picture is not worth a thousand words, but a thousand confusions. Oh, and we've all experienced the autocorrect fail. *"How's your day going?"* compared to the autocorrect *"How's your dad going?"* can leave your love interest confused, thinking you care more about their parents than them. Navigating this maze of miscommunication requires patience, a sense of humor, or just a good old-fashioned phone call to clear the air.

Fear of intimacy

Fear of intimacy in the digital dating world adds a complex layer to the already intricate process of building genuine connections. In a realm where relationships often start with a swipe of a message, this fear can manifest in unique ways, profoundly influencing how people interact and bond. Many stick to light, superficial interactions, and surface-level conversations online, steering clear of deeper, more meaningful exchanges. This can be partly due to fear of becoming too vulnerable with someone they've never met in person. Chats often hover around hobbies and interests without delving into personal beliefs, feelings, or fears. In addition, without the full spectrum of non-verbal cues and real-time interaction, people tend to fill in the gaps with their imagination. This can lead to idealizing a potential partner based on limited information shared online, projecting qualities onto them that might not truly exist. Here, there is no real intimacy, just perceived closeness. Fear of intimacy might lead some to ghosting or withdrawal when things start to get too real, or emotions become too intense. Unfortunately, this stops genuine connections from forming, as ghosting leaves the other person confused and more guarded against future interactions. Conversely, some might respond to fear of intimacy by oversharing personal information too early in the relationship. This can be an unconscious attempt to test the waters and see if the other person can handle their "worst" upfront. However, it can overwhelm the recipient and push them away.

The culture of instant gratification

In a world where people can get almost anything with a swipe or a click from food delivery to a ride across town, expectations for immediate results have seeped into how we approach relationships, often to their detriment. Digital dating platforms are designed to provide quick matches, offering users an array of potential partners within minutes. The ease of finding new connections can devalue individual interactions, as people may feel there is always another option just a swipe away. The result is a reluctance to invest time and effort into any relationship, hindering the development of deeper connections. The instant communication enabled by digital platforms can also contribute to superficial connections. Continuous messing can create a false sense of intimacy and urgency that pressures people to share personal details prematurely or fabricate emotional investments that do not truly feel. The ease of meeting new people online can also lead to a culture of disposable relationships, where people may quickly abandon connections at the first sight of conflict or incompatibility, rather than working through issues. This behavior limits the depth of relationships, as it avoids the challenges and growth that strengthen bonds.

Fear of vulnerability

Fear of vulnerability is a significant barrier in the world of digital dating, where the perceived safety of the screen often encourages superficial interactions rather than deep emotional engagement. This fear can severely limit the development of genuine connections, as individuals may hold back their true selves or shy away from deeper discussions. Many people use their digital persona to present an idealized version of themselves, curating profiles that highlight only their most attractive qualities and accomplishments. This selective sharing is driven by the fear of being judged or rejected for one's flaws or deeper emotional needs. People fearing vulnerability often steer conversations toward safe, non-intimate topics. Discussions about personal fears, past relationships, or deep emotional wounds are avoided. The transition from online chatting to in-person meetings is a significant step that requires vulnerability. Those who fear this exposure often find reasons to delay or avoid meeting, which can stagnate the relationship and prevent the kind of interactions that deepen connections, such as physical touch and eye contact.

The Love Lighthouse Principle - A Guide to Finding Genuine Online Connections

Just as sailors use lighthouses to guide them safely to shore, you can use the Love Lighthouse Principle to navigate the turbulent sea of digital love. The Love Lighthouse Principle is simple yet powerful. It's all about being your authentic self, radiating positivity, and attracting those who appreciate your unique light. The idea that a lighthouse is a beacon that attracts the right kind of ships (partners) by shining its light authentically and steadily can be explained in several ways:

Shine your Authentic Light

The first step in the Love Lighthouse Principle is about authenticity. Just as a lighthouse doesn't change its light to suit the ships, you should not alter your core self to attract a partner. It encourages honesty. In a realm where people might hide behind masks, being truthful about who you are can be refreshing and magnetic. For instance, instead of pretending to love hiking to match with an outdoorsy person, openly sharing your love for cozy reading nooks might attract someone who shares and respects your interests. The goal is to attract those who are genuinely aligned with your authentic self. According to a scientific study, it was found that people who exercise authenticity in their lives tend to lead better lives with stable psychological health and better relationships (Goldman, B. M., & Kernis, M. H, 2002).

Use your Light to Guide, Not Blind

This emphasizes positivity. Just as a lighthouse shine bright amid darkness, your positive attitude can pierce through the gloom of negativity that often clouds online interactions. By focusing on what makes you happy and sharing those experiences online, you draw people who resonate with your joy. It's important to guide potential partners toward understanding who you are and what you need positively without overwhelming them. For example, sharing your passion for cooking could inspire a foodie to reach out, sparking conversations filled with shared enthusiasm.

Stay Steady Amidst the Storms

Navigating online dating can be tumultuous with rejections, miscommunications, and disappointments akin to storms at sea. The Love Lighthouse stands firm regardless of the weather, symbolizing resilience in your dating journey. It's about maintaining your standards and values, even when things get tough, ensuring you don't compromise just to avoid being alone.

Scan the Horizon

A lighthouse scans the horizon, not just to be seen, but also to see. In the context of digital dating, this means being proactive in seeking out potential partners who share your values and interests, but also being observant and discerning about the signs and signals you receive from others. Be open to noticing who is responsive to your authentic self and who reciprocates your level of commitment and interest. Talk about your likes and dislikes and share your deal-breakers as well.

Maintain your Energy Source.

Just as a lighthouse needs a reliable energy source to keep shining, maintaining your emotional and mental well-being is crucial in the digital dating world. This involves managing your expectations, not investing too soon, and ensuring you have a fulfilling life outside of dating. This self-care ensures your light doesn't dim. There is no need to rush into anything.

The Love Lighthouse Principle provides a strategic and heart-centered approach to digital dating. By embodying the qualities of a lighthouse – authenticity, visibility, discernment, and self-sufficiency you can increase your chances of finding meaningful connections in the digital age. This principle isn't just about finding a partner; it's about attracting the kind of relationship that is enriching, stable, and right for you. The ultimate goal is not just to attract any ship, but to guide the right ones into safe harbor - a genuine, meaningful connection.

Chapter 14:
Disconnected Connections: Breakups on Social Media

Breaking up is like knocking over a Coke machine. You can't do it with one push – you got to rock it back and forth a few times, and then it goes over. – Jerry Seinfeld

In the digital age, breaking up doesn't just mean parting ways with your partner; it also means potentially losing your hashtag squad, your meme-sharing compadres, and those delightful online friends who have been rooting for your relationship from behind their screens. Things take a turn for the worse when a relationship that bloomed once changes its status (Blackburn & Brody, n.d.).

So, when you hit "end" on a romantic textationship, you might also face the dreaded "unfollow" apocalypse across your social media universe. Welcome to the digital disaster zone – where your heart isn't the only thing left on "read." Remember when people used to tear up love letters, throw away gifts, and burn up pictures of their ex-partners to get over them? The saying "Out of sight, out of mind"? Yeah. That doesn't really work anymore. Even though I am sure doing all of this brings great satisfaction, it doesn't really help you forget and erase someone from your life completely. Why, you might ask? The answer is simple.

Social media.

And this, my friend, is where the internet-based support

system makes an entry. An internet-based support system is not your grandma's shoulder that you can cry on or your best friend's stash of cookies and ice cream that you can rely on. No, this is when your army of digital friends and followers—and even random strangers—swoop in to make you feel better or often worse.

In this chapter, we will delve into the details of how social media has become both a lifeline and an emotional landmine after a breakup.

Navigating Shared Spaces Post-Breakup

Social media can amplify the emotional distress of a breakup. Regular updates from or about an ex can make moving on harder. Seeing pictures of an ex looking seemingly happy can trigger feelings of jealousy or loneliness. The public nature of social media can also exacerbate these feelings because the breakup isn't just a private matter: it's out there for friends (or the public) to see and possibly comment on. You might find yourself questioning, "To block or not to block?" Should you unfollow or just mute? Should you post, or is it too soon? And the most important one, should you change your relationship status? Navigating shared spaces online post-breakup can be emotionally taxing. A study shows that after a breakup, the behavior of people on Facebook changes accordingly. Around 22.7% of people hide or remove their relationship status while 10.2% resort to stalking their exes (LeFebvre, L., Blackburn, K., & Brody, N, 2015).

The accessibility of an ex's online activity leads many to monitor their social media. This behavior can become compulsive, hindering emotional recovery. There you are one minute having a good day, and then one picture of your ex with their arm around another person can have you reeling toward a sobbing mess.

Social media posts are often curated, only showing the best aspects of someone's life. Post-breakup, individuals may overanalyze these snippets, misconstruing them as true representations of their ex's feelings or new life without them. This can lead to unnecessary pain and prolong the healing process. Additionally, there's an unspoken notion of needing to "win" the breakup by appearing to move on faster or by being the first to show you're doing great. The pressure can prompt people to post content that is aimed at getting a reaction from an ex, rather than genuine expressions of moving on.

Disconnect to Reconnect - Taking a Hiatus from Social Media

When a gardener notices a plant struggling to thrive, he doesn't just toss extra fertilizer its way hoping for the best. Instead, he takes time to prune the dead limbs, repot them in fresh soil, and give them a break from harsh sunlight. This process of rejuvenation can be likened to you deciding to take a social media hiatus following a breakup. Deciding to disconnect from social media is like pruning the dead limbs. It clears away the noise, the constant updates, and the barrage of emotions that come with watching an ex-partner move on virtually. It allows you to focus on healing and growth, without being haunted by digital ghosts.

For example, Sara, a 32-year-old graphic designer, found peace in deleting her social media apps post-breakup. She reported feeling less anxious and more present in her day-to-day life.

Replanting in fresh soil is like rediscovering your interests outside of the digital realm. When you're not spending hours scrolling through feeds, you have time to reignite old hobbies or learn new ones.

Think about Mike, a music teacher who took a two-month social media hiatus and rekindled his love for hiking and nature photography.

Giving the plant a break from harsh sunlight is synonymous with escaping the glare of public scrutiny that social media often brings. Without the pressure to seem 'okay' or portray an idealized version of your life post-break-up, you're free to truly heal at your own pace.

This was the case for Emma, a writer who felt liberated when she stopped crafting perfect captions for her Instagram posts during her social media break.

Disconnecting from social media after a breakup isn't about running away – this involves creating a safe space for personal growth and healing. It helps reduce the temptation to check up on your ex and can minimize unnecessary emotional triggers. This sounds like one of the most difficult things ever, but trust me, the world won't end if you don't know what your ex had for lunch or who they're hanging out with on a Friday night. In fact, you might just find that the world outside of your phone screen is much richer and more fulfilling than you remember. It's not about losing connections but about reconnecting with yourself and the world around you. The first thing to do after you get out of a relationship is to make yourself your biggest priority.

Taking a hiatus from social media following a breakup can be transformative, empowering you to navigate through your healing journey at your own pace. It is a testament to the resilience of the human spirit, and its ability to thrive when given the right environment – just like the plant in the gardener's care.

Blocking Out Negativity - To Block or Not to Block?

Slapping a Band-Aid on a wound? That's practically a reflex. And when the wound is heart-shaped, blocking your ex on social media might seem like a go-to quick fix to stop the bleeding. But is it the most effective way to heal? In today's digital era, relationships extend beyond the physical realm. They weave through the virtual threads of our social media accounts, becoming intertwined with our daily online activities. When these relationships end, their digital imprints stay, often making it difficult to move on.

To block or not to block – that is the question.

Blocking an ex-partner on social media platforms is one-way people try to navigate this challenge. However, it's not always as straightforward as it seems. Blocking can provide immediate relief from the onslaught of post-breakup emotions. It's like turning off a faucet that's been pouring out reminders of a life once shared. You no longer have to see their new posts or mutual friends tagging them in photos – just sweet, sweet digital silence. It's an instant breather for your heart and your homepage.

Secondly, blocking can establish clear boundaries, especially if the breakup is messy. It sends a direct message to your ex-partner that you need space and time to heal. This can prevent unnecessary confrontations or awkward conversations that could further complicate things.

In addition, blocking can help you regain control over your online space. After a breakup, it's essential to rebuild a safe environment where you feel comfortable expressing yourself. By controlling who has access to your posts and personal information, you can start shaping this space to reflect your individuality and growth.

However, blocking isn't always the best option for everyone. Sometimes, it might feel like an overreaction or an act of hostility. Other times, it might not align with your healing process or personal beliefs. What if they want to reach out? What if they want to discuss something important with you in the future? And, hey, you are no coward, so why should you block them? Does all of this sound familiar? It's important to remember that there is no one-size-fits-all approach to post-breakup recovery. Worry not because I have the perfect solution for you: a block or no block pro and con list (Bijan, 2023)!

Pros

1. Out of sight, out of mind. The less you see them, the easier it will be to move on.

2. You save yourself the trouble of seeing their new partners.

3. You don't even have to worry about them reaching out to you.

4. You get to avoid any mind games or guilt-tripping by keeping them away.

5. There is no chance of drunk dialing them or reaching out in your weak moments.

Cons

1. You might come across as petty or even insensitive.

2. You will lose the opportunity to have any kind of bond with that person.

3. You will become completely unaware of all the big events that happen in their life.

4. This might be enough of a sign for people to understand that you have broken up, even though you want to keep it private.

5. They won't see you moving on.

When it comes down to it, deciding whether to block or not to block is a personal decision that should be made based on your individual needs and circumstances. It's a tool available to you, but it's not the only tool. In the grand web of online connections, managing your virtual circle post-breakup is key. Whether you decide to block, mute, or simply scroll on by, it's your call. So, curate it as you please, and let the healing begin.

Chapter 15:

Rebuilding Self-Esteem After Digital Dating Dilemmas

What lies behind us and what lies before us are tiny matters compared to what lies within us. – Ralph Waldo Emerson

Rebuilding your self-esteem after a digital dating dilemma is an opportunity for rebirth and renewal. It's about dusting off the negativity, standing tall, and moving forward with newfound strength and wisdom. Understand that self-esteem isn't something that can be shattered beyond repair. It's not a delicate glass figurine but rather a resilient rubber ball. Remember that your worth is not defined by your digital dating experiences. If someone doesn't appreciate your value, it doesn't diminish your worth – it simply means they failed to see it.

You're an uncut gem, and just because someone can't spot your sparkle doesn't mean you don't shine, baby. Remember, every misfire on the dating app is like a bad experiment in a lab – you're just tweaking the formula until you hit that relationship Eureka!

It's crucial to learn from these experiences rather than letting them define you. Every failed online date or unsatisfying conversation becomes a steppingstone towards gaining better understanding of what you truly seek in a partner.

Navigating love in the age of swipes and likes can make anyone feel a bit down. But let's not let a bunch of pixels pull us down, right? Remember, just as you wouldn't judge a book by its cover, don't let online interactions determine your self-worth. Rebuilding self-esteem after Digital Dating Dilemmas is like refining gold – the process may be tough, but the end result is pure and priceless. So chin up, and forward march. There's a whole lot of fabulous you to be discovered, with or without Wi-Fi!

Understanding Self-Esteem

Self-esteem takes time to build but can be shattered in an instant, especially after something as emotionally charged as a breakup. Self-esteem is more than just feeling good about yourself. It's a crucial part of our psychological makeup that influences our behavior, thoughts, and feelings. When you've been through a breakup, particularly one that originated from digital dating, your self-esteem can take a serious hit.

Self-esteem affects our resilience. When you have healthy self-esteem, you're better equipped to bounce back after setbacks. Think about the last time you faced rejection on a dating app. Did it knock you down for weeks or were you able to brush it off and keep swiping? Our self-esteem is intertwined with our mental health. Studies show that low self-esteem can lead to problems like depression and anxiety. For example, constantly comparing your own life to the picture-perfect moments people share online can trigger feelings of inadequacy and discontent. Self-esteem impacts our relationships. It determines how we interact with others and how we let others treat us. On the other hand, it can also be a superhero cape that you throw on and suddenly you trust yourself to conquer the whole world.

In simpler words, self-esteem is how we perceive ourselves. You are the captain of your own boat. Your entire life depends on what you think you deserve and how you view yourself. And that has a huge impact on how you lead your life. In fact, it affects several parts of your life, including the following (Mind, n.d.):

1. Whether you like yourself or not.
2. Whether you think of yourself as worthy of good things.
3. Your ability to not blame yourself for things you didn't do.
4. Your ability to trust yourself to make the right decisions.
5. Your ability to recognize when others should treat you well.

If you think poorly of yourself, you'll likely settle for less than what you deserve in partnerships or online dating scenarios. You might accept neglect, disrespect, or abuse because you believe that's all you are worth. In essence, our self-esteem is the compass that guides us through life's various terrains. It's not merely about feeling good about ourselves – this involves recognizing our inherent worth and navigating through life with a sense of dignity and respect for oneself.

When we learn to master this internal compass, we can steer clear of the pitfalls of low self-esteem and chart a course towards healthier relationships, improved performance, and overall well-being. Remember, the battle with self-esteem is often unseen, but its impact is profoundly felt in every aspect of our lives.

Self-Love Practices for Inner Healing

Just as a gardener tends to their plants, providing them with the right amount of sunlight, water, and nutrients, so too should we tend to our own emotional health. This is where the practice of self-love comes into play, serving as the sunlight, water, and nutrients for our emotional well-being.

Self-love is about a lot more than just taking bubble baths or treating yourself to a shopping spree. It's a deeper process that involves recognizing your worth, honoring your boundaries, and nurturing your emotional health. The digital dating dilemmas we've covered in previous chapters can take a toll on your self-esteem if you're not grounded in self-love. By cultivating an inner sanctuary of love and respect for yourself, you become resilient in the face of these digital dilemmas.

For example, imagine you've been chatting with someone online and they suddenly stop responding. If you're grounded in self-love, instead of spiraling into self-doubt, you'll be able to remind yourself that their actions are a reflection of them, not your worth. The practice of self-love is not a one-time event, but a continuous path. It's about consistently showing up for yourself every single day, even when it's hard, even when you don't feel like it like you would for your friends (Healing Holidays, n.d.).

You are the main character of your life. Make your mind, your soul, and your body your priority. Commit to a relationship with yourself by:

1. Self-Discovery: Take the time to understand your values, dreams, and desires. This self-awareness lays the foundation for authentic connections with others.

2. Self-Worth: Prioritize self-care and compassion. When you love yourself, you establish a strong emotional foundation that enhances the quality of your relationships.

3. Independence: Cultivate independence and learn to rely on yourself. This empowers you to contribute fully to a partnership without losing your sense of self.

4. Healthy Boundaries: Establishing boundaries is key to any successful relationship. By understanding your own limits and needs, you can communicate them effectively to others.

5. Personal Growth: A commitment to yourself means a commitment to personal growth. Continuously strive to be the best version of yourself, fostering resilience and adaptability.

Self-love is not a luxury, it's a necessity. Just as the gardener's plants flourish with the right care, so too will your emotional health with the practice of self-love. In a book called *Authentic Self-Love: A Path to Healing the Self and Relationships* by Sepideh Irvani, self-love is described as a crucial part of our lives, and when people suffer through the absence of self-love, it tends to clash with their entire identity and all of their relationships. This makes healing even more difficult (*Authentic Self-Love*, n.d.). In relation to that, a study found that self-affirmation enhances our performance and makes us more receptive to our mistakes (Silverman et al., 2013).

In our digital age where online dating dilemmas are common, self-love becomes our shield and our beacon, leading us towards healthier relationships and inner healing.

Get Your Groove Back – Regaining Your Power After a Digital Dating Disaster

Let's face it, getting back to normal after a particularly disastrous relationship that left your self-esteem in shambles is like trying to assemble furniture without any instructions. Everything is a mess, and you have no idea where to begin.

Too many people give their power away in online relationships because they never learned how to value themselves. They'll freeze their whole life, staring at their phone, waiting for a 'ping' that could just be an app update. They drop their dreams faster than a hot potato for a lukewarm relationship. Chasing the emotionally unavailable as if it's a sport, basically saying "pick me" for their team in a high school game of dodgeball. They say yes when they want to say no. They don't communicate for fear of pushing someone away. And oh, they hand out second chances to people who probably didn't deserve the first one.

Feeling desired is like getting a flame emoji on social media:

instant gratification, but fleeting. Being valued, though? This means they seek to know you deeply, learn your story, and actively engage in communication. They make efforts to include you in their plans and discuss future possibilities together.

But remember, it's crucial to value yourself first.

This self-respect empowers you to step away from those who might desire you but don't genuinely value your presence. Someone who treats you like a quick like rather than a long-term subscribe? Nope, that's a no from you.

Steps towards practicing self-respect to get your power back:

1. **Flaunt Your Flaws**

No one is perfect – not even those seemingly flawless profiles you come across online! Celebrate your quirks, they're your personal trademarks.

2. **Cultivate Positive Relationships**

Surround yourself with people who uplift and encourage you rather than those who drain your energy. Hang with cheerleaders, not energy vampires. Positive vibes only!

3. **Invest in Yourself**

Whether that means taking up a new hobby or investing in personal development courses, spend time and resources on improving yourself. New skills, new experiences, new you!

4. **Zen Your Way Through the Day**

Stay present in each moment instead of dwelling on past failures or worrying about future outcomes. Live in the now. Yesterday's ghosts don't deserve your energy today.

Self-love and self-respect are about more than just feeling good about yourself. It's about appreciating your worth and taking actions that reflect this self-respect. Remember, it's ok to take a break from dating if you need to. This doesn't mean you're giving up on love – it simply means you're prioritizing your mental health and well-being over the pursuit of a romantic relationship. Your journey back to self-love and confidence is not just about recovery; it's about thriving and recognizing your inherent worth. Keep these lessons close to heart and watch how they transform not only your view of yourself but also how you interact with the world around you. I promise you, when you are your own biggest fan, life becomes a whole lot more fun.

Chapter 16:

Healing Journey

The wound is the place where the light enters you. - Rumi

Ever felt like you're on a relationship relay race, sprinting from one partner to the next without catching a breath? One moment you're swiping left on a string of disappointing profiles, and the next, you're jumping headfirst into a new relationship that seems promising but ultimately ends up being just another setback in your quest for love. It's like you're running from one train to catch the next without even stopping to think if it's the right one for you. The distraction of a new love interest can be a tempting one, as it helps you avoid the pain and sadness from the relationship that just ended. But have you ever wondered if this rush of getting into a new relationship might be causing you more harm than good? This pattern can take a toll on your emotional well-being.

When a relationship ends, it can be a hurricane of heartache – confusion, sadness, a splash of anger, and a whole lot of "What just happened?" vibes. It's rough. Yet, instead of dealing with all those messy feelings, some of us are ready to swipe right into the sunset of someone new. We think it's a painkiller, but it's more like putting a Band-Aid on a broken leg. Imagine you're in a shiny new relationship, but oops, you've brought your old emotional luggage along for the ride. How do you break it to your new bae that your heart is still bruised from your ex? Sure, they might understand at first, but who wants a plus-one encroaching on a budding relationship? Skipping the emotional homework doesn't make the underlying issues vanish. They are just going to resurface and crash your love life's party later. It's like ignoring a check engine light and hoping your car won't break down on the freeway.

There's a way out – embarking on a healing journey.

Embarking on a healing journey after these romantic misadventures isn't just about licking your wounds – it's about turning those wounds into wisdom. Take a moment to reflect on the montage of mismatches and missed connections. Were you chasing a fairy tale instead of seeking real compatibility? Each ghosting and fizzled fling may leave a mark, but these aren't just emotional bruises: they're badges of honor (or at least they can be).

Your healing journey plays a critical role in various aspects of your life. First, it provides an opportunity to reflect on past relationships. Reflecting helps you identify patterns and behaviors that may have contributed to your dating disappointments. For instance, you might realize that you've been prioritizing potential over compatibility, leading to unfulfilled relationships. Secondly, this journey gives you the chance to heal from emotional wounds. Every swipe left or heartbreak leaves a scar. Healing allows you to acknowledge these scars, understand their impact, and start working towards recovery. Finally, this isn't just about recovery. Healing boosts your self-esteem and arms you with resilience so robust, that you might find yourself thanking your past flings for their contribution to your growth – gratitude instead of grudges!

Remember, healing is not a linear process. There will be ups and downs, moments of clarity and moments of doubt. Embrace them all as part of your path.

So, let your wounds be the gateway toward healing!

Tools for Building Positive Future Relationships

In order to build positive and enduring future relationships, you need to equip yourself with some invaluable tools—tools that empower you to navigate the twists and turns of love with clarity and grace. Here are some of the tools that can help you get on the path toward lasting and fulfilling connections:

Self-awareness: Understanding your need in a relationship

Self-awareness is the ability to understand, perceive, and recognize the things that make you a unique individual. It encompasses the awareness of your thoughts, emotions, attitude, beliefs, values, actions, and your whole personality.

Self-awareness isn't just essential for yourself but for your relationships as well. It's hard to share the aspects of yourself with someone else when you're unaware of your own strengths and weaknesses. Getting into a relationship without a deep understanding of oneself and one's needs often leads to confusion and conflicts. Self-awareness helps us gain insight into our desires, fears, and boundaries which are important when it comes to building a healthy relationship.

Though it takes time to develop the habit of self-reflecting and self-evaluation, you need to prioritize it for your own well-being and to develop positive relationships.

Communication: A key tool in building relationship

Communication is the lifeline of any thriving relationship. It's like the glue that holds the relationship together. If you want to effectively communicate with your partner, you need to learn two things: active listening and clearly expressing yourself.

When you really listen to someone, it shows them that you genuinely care and respect what they have to say. It helps you develop trust in your relationship. Similarly, when you express yourself clearly, you make sure that your thoughts and feelings are understood. This helps prevent misunderstandings and conflicts. So, by listening actively and expressing yourself clearly, you can create an atmosphere where your relationship can grow stronger with every passing day.

Setting boundaries in a relationship

Setting boundaries is a vital aspect of every healthy relationship. Boundaries serve as the fences around our emotional garden that not only protect our well-being but preserve our autonomy as well. By describing what is acceptable and what isn't, we can create a safe space for intimacy to flourish that is free from misunderstandings and resentments.

But don't just take my word—scientific studies have also highlighted the importance of boundary-setting in fostering relationship satisfaction. A study in 2018 underscored the correlation between clear boundaries and mutual respect, highlighting the pivotal role they play in nurturing a satisfactory connection (Marcello et al., 2018).

Celebrating Growth and Progress on Your Healing Journey

Think back to a time when you were a child learning to ride a bike. Each time you managed to pedal a little farther without falling, you felt a sense of achievement. This is not so different from your blueprint that leads toward healing from a digital dating disappointment.

The Power of Small Wins

Acknowledging mini-victories is essential. First, it cultivates self-compassion. Just as you wouldn't belittle a child for not being able to pedal across the park on their first try, don't criticize yourself for not moving on immediately post-breakup. For instance, you might find that you're able to go an hour without checking your ex's social media. Even though it's a small step, it's still progress.

Secondly, celebrating the small wins helps build momentum.

Remember when pedaling your bike felt nearly impossible, but after a few successful tries, you started to believe you could? The same principle applies here. Maybe today you only cried once instead of three times. That is progress and deserves acknowledgement. Lastly, these micro-victories can serve as a beacon of hope during dark times. Just like the first time you rode your bike without training wheels, these moments remind you that healing is possible and within reach. These are the signs that you are on your way to recovery.

Recognizing these mini milestones might seem insignificant in the grand scheme of things, but remember, even the longest journey begins with a single step - it takes time and comes in baby steps. That's brave, my friend! So, take a moment to pat yourself on the back! Celebrating the small victories in your healing journey is like adding bricks to your recovery foundation. Each brick might seem insignificant on its own, but together they create a solid base that can withstand future storms.

So, don't dismiss these moments.

Instead cherish them, because they are the steppingstones leading you towards a stronger you. By acknowledging and celebrating our successes, we fuel our sense of accomplishment and boost our motivation to persevere. From hitting a new milestone in self-care to embarking on an adventure of solitude, each win serves as a testament to our resilience and determination. Research has also recognized the power of small wins. The well-known academics Teresa Amabile and Steven J. Kramer highlighted that small wins can really enhance our inner life, boosting our self-esteem and motivation (Amabile & Kramer, 2011).

Healthy Practice for Future Online Relationships

In this vast digital sea, it's easy to get swept away by the currents of excitement and novelty. But remember; honesty, communication, and boundaries are your compass, your map, and your life jacket. They will guide you to the shores of a healthy and fulfilling online relationship. Online dating has the potential to connect us in ways we could never have imagined. But like any tool, it must be used responsibly.

So, if you are ready to dive into the wild world of digital dating again? Let me equip you with some dating etiquette and safety measures, to make you the master of dating platforms:

Online Dating Etiquette

- Communication matters – Good communication goes beyond well-crafted messages. This involves timing too. Avoid keeping someone waiting for days without a response or bombard them with constant texts. If you don't feel a connection or wish to end things, simply say it out loud. Don't disappear into thin air. Oh, and please don't use copy-and-paste pick-up lines in your profile. By the way "Hey" is not communication.

- Respect boundaries – Everyone has their own boundaries. Respect them just as much as you want yours respected. And if you're not genuinely interested in someone, don't string them along. Respect their time and feelings, and end things on time before it's too late.

- Privacy Protection – Protecting personal information should be a priority when engaging in online dating activities. Never feel obliged to share personal information if you don't feel comfortable.

- Honesty is key – Honesty forms the foundation of any relationship, even those formed online. Represent yourself accurately in your profile. Nobody wants to show up for a date and discover their "6 feet tall, outdoor enthusiast" match is actually a "5'7, Netflix binger."

- Handle Rejection Gracefully -If someone has enough guts to tell you that they're not interested, accept it gracefully, move on, and look for another match. Don't pressure or harass anyone after being rejected.

Safety Measures When Using Online Dating Apps

- Choose a well-known, reputable dating app with robust safety features and policies in place.

- Be cautious of profiles with limited information or suspicious details.

- Don't share sensitive information with someone until you're comfortable enough and have established trust with them.

- Don't share revealing or explicit photos as they can be

misused or distributed without your consent.

- When meeting someone in person, choose a public place and tell your friend your whereabouts. Prioritize your safety at all costs.

Conclusion

Online dating: where socially awkward people can be socially awkward together...but separately...in their own homes –Unknown

Ah, what a whirlwind journey we've embarked upon through the labyrinth of digital dating! As we've come so far, standing at the crossroads of love, loss, and learning in this digital age, let's reflect on the tales we shared and the lessons we've learned.

First, the heart still reigns supreme, even in a world where you might be judged by a poorly chosen profile pic or an unfortunate autocorrect. Secondly, we've discovered that while ghosting should probably be left to specters, the art of crafting a perfect text should not be underestimated. Who knew that punctuation could be so powerful? A well-placed exclamation point might be the difference between a second date and a 'seen' message. From the highs of love bombing to the lows of ghosting, and the haunting paths of gaslighting, catfishing, and breadcrumbing in between, we've witnessed the twists and turns of modern romance. And what could now guide us better than the story of my dear friend, Andrea, whose misadventures in the digital dating realm are a nutshell of what we've learned so far?

Now, picture this: Andrea, was innocently scrolling through her Instagram DM requests, when suddenly a message pops up on her screen: "Remember me?" Cue the intrigue, the mystery, the curiosity of digital romance!

Andrea, who admits to having a sea of suitors, decides to take this bait and respond. Well, time moved on, and this guy's turned on the **rizz** with flirtatious and charming messages flooding her inbox with compliments and promises of love like no other. Ah, yes, she was being **love-bombed**. But all is not as it seems in the land of digital love. Andrea soon discovered that he was not quite single. Oh no, is he **roaching**? Yep! He was entangled in the web of another relationship with a girl named Marla, who coincidentally, she knew as an acquaintance. He tried to assure Andrea that he would entangle himself soon enough because he and Marla were really only friends, that it was Marla who liked him. The kicker is that he told Andrea to keep their relationship a secret (**stashing**) from Marla to not hurt her feelings. And like a moth to a flame, Andrea was drawn further into the deception, keeping their love story under wraps like a secret from Marla.

Here enters the twist: Marla was entangled in the same web of deceit. He was **benching** her, looking for someone else while dating her. Oh, the irony! But guess what? Instead of confronting her dastardly suitor, Andrea fell for the illusion while desperately wanting to make this digital dalliance work. Little did she know what was coming next for her. When she gathered some evidence that he was actually romantically dating Marla and dared to confront him, guess what was waiting for her? The denial, the dismissal, the manipulation—yes, he started **gaslighting** Andrea with comments like, "*You're wrong*," "*Your jealousy is giving **ick**,*" and "*You're overreacting.*" The audacity, man!

But wait, things didn't end here—there's more! Just when Andrea started distancing herself from his digital grip because she knew the truth, he reeled back in with sweet nothings and fake promises. Hot and cold, on and off—the **breadcrumb** of his fake affection led her deeper into the darkness of deception.

And then when he could no longer deny his pack of lies, the final blow—blocked, **ghosted**, vanished into thin air, and Andrea was left with unanswered questions. And there you have it—Digital Dating Dilemmas...Deception, Disasters, Disillusions, Disappointments! The list goes on...

As we gaze into the future, we glimpse the tantalizing possibilities of AI, VR, and beyond in the realm of digital dating. These advancements will bring salvation and further turmoil, only time will tell!

But don't worry because even in chaos and heartache, there's always a beacon of hope. Yet, in admitting the ever-changing landscape of love, let's not forget the timeless virtues that guide us: communication, honesty, respect, and self-awareness. So, whether you swipe right or left, navigate algorithms or avatars, these virtues are our true companions in the quest for love. In the end, whether we swipe left, swipe right, or just double-tap our way through the complexities of digital love, the quest for human connection remains as enduring as ever. As we log off, let's remember the true message of our digital dating dilemma: in a world where you can be anyone online, the bravest thing you can be is yourself. Authenticity might just be the key to unlocking a connection that's more than skin-deep, or screen-deep.

Here's to finding love in a hopeless place – online and off. May your Wi-Fi be strong, your dates be kind, and your romantic entanglements be few. And remember, the next time you find yourself despairing over the digital dating dilemmas, there's always the option to close the app and meet someone the old-fashioned way – in the real world.

So, keep calm and swipe on!

Glossary of 50 Modern-Day Terms

Ah, the modern world, always evolving. And you know what's the most exhausting part of this new trend-setting generation? The terms that we have to keep up with. There is an array of terms that might be difficult for some to catch onto. And for that, here is a glossary to make your life easier:

1. **Beige flag:** An inoffensive term for people who are boring.
2. **Benching:** Just like in football, in dating terms, this means keeping someone on the sideline while you explore other options, and if you find none, you might turn to them from time to time.
3. **Breadcrumbing:** This is when someone gives you some attention; small crumbs here and there instead of being serious. People tend to do this to keep people interested without any intention of dating them.
4. **Caspering:** Ever heard of "Casper the Ghost"? He is known for being a friendly ghost, so the people who inform their partners that they will be going away for a while are given the term Casper.
5. **Catch and release:** The typical playboys who are obsessed with the thrill of chasing someone and catching them. Feels like a big achievement to them and an easy ego boost.
6. **Catfishing:** When you see pictures of a model on someone's dating profile, you have caught a catfisher. These are people who pretend to be someone they aren't.
7. **Cobwebbing:** A process of getting rid of any thoughts of your ex by ridding yourself of any memories or objects you might have of theirs.

8. **Cookie jarring:** It's like having your two feet in two different boats. This is when people keep an eye out for someone else in hopes of dating them as a backup.
9. **Cricketing:** When you text someone and they leave you on read instead of responding.
10. **Cuffing season:** The shift of season between summers and winters that makes people yearn for long-term companionship rather than casual flings.
11. **Curve:** When someone avoids any commitment or relationship while continuing to respond to texts. They want to seem nice, but their replies are sporadic and filled with lame excuses for why they can't meet up.
12. **Cushioning:** AKA your backup plan. This happens when you maintain flirtatious conversations with others as a backup in case your current relationship fails.
13. **DTR:** Short for "Define the relationship," the three words that most commitment-phobes are terrified of. A conversation that leads to discussing the status and expectations of a relationship.
14. **Eclipsing:** You ever had a friend who started doing everything their partner did? Same hobbies, same interests, same likes and dislikes. Yep, that's eclipsing for you.
15. **Fauxbae'ing:** Fooling someone into believing they are dating when in reality they aren't.
16. **Fleabagging:** When people self-sabotage their relationships because of their own insecurities and troubles, like a fear of intimacy. This term was taken from the titular character in the show *Fleabag*.
17. **Flexting:** The perfect recipe for impressing people (or so they think). Flexters are the ones who exaggerate their lifestyles and everything else to impress potential partners.
18. **Flying monkeys:** Taking after the monkeys in *The*

Wizard of Oz—who are the ones carrying out all the dirty work, in case you didn't know—this term is associated with someone who is recruited by a toxic person to disrupt someone else's life.

19. **Freckling:** Just like your freckles fade as summer slips away, your relationship does too.
20. **Gaslighting:** Typically happens when someone doesn't take accountability for their actions but instead blames you for their mistakes, making you question your own perception of the event.
21. **Ghostbusting:** Have you ever met someone who can't seem to accept that they have been ghosted? Ghostbusting is when someone continues to call someone who is ghosting them.
22. **Ghosting:** The typical peek-a-boo game for you. This tends to occur when someone out of the blue vanishes without any explanation whatsoever.
23. **Groundhogging:** People who decide they want to stick to one type rather than explore other options, so they find similar partners but with expectations for a better relationship.
24. **Haunting:** Liking your stories and your posts to make their existence known without initiating any direct conversation.
25. **Hoovering:** Basically the unwanted return of an abusive ex who wants you again.
26. **Ick:** An immediate turn off because of an action or behavior of someone you were interested in, like the way someone eats on social media.
27. **IRL:** Short for "in real life," this is used to distinguish between online interactions and real-life ones.
28. **Kittenfishing:** Quite similar to catfishing but on a lower scale, as in this case, the person is real but they act in an unrealistic way, knowing that that isn't how

they are in real life.

29. **Left on read:** The same as cricketing; when someone sees your message and ignores it.
30. **Love bombing:** Has anyone ever said the three magical words to you in the first week of dating? Congratulations, you have been love-bombed! Showering someone with excessive love, affection, and attention very quickly is love bombing.
31. **Marleying:** Christmas season and a text from your ex? Who else is surprised that you are a victim of marleying?
32. **Mosting:** This one is quite similar to love bombing, only a little less intense, and doesn't happen for more than two or three days before they start ignoring you.
33. **Orbiting:** We all have that one person who constantly and actively interacts with all your posts but never initiates a conversation. That is what orbiters do.
34. **Peacocking:** You ever feel like someone is being too much? Peacocking is when someone tries too hard by dressing attractively and portraying talents to impress others.
35. **Phubbing:** Nobody likes a phubber. Why? Well, who likes someone who chooses to use their phone or other electronic device while ignoring you? And that's exactly what phubbing is.
36. **Rizz:** The pick-up lines, the charm, and the flirtatious comments are all now classified as rizz.
37. **Roaching:** Don't you just hate finding roaches in a dirty apartment? Yeah, well, in the same manner, anyone would hate roaching, which is finding their partner involved with other romantic partners.
38. **Serendipidating:** Has someone ever constantly bailed on a plan, asking to reschedule? That is exactly what serendipidating is: they hold a date off in case they

might come across someone better.

39. **Shaveducking:** This one is silly but hey, I don't judge! This is when you are paranoid that you only like someone because of their beard.
40. **Sidebarring:** This happens when you are on a date but you can't help but be more invested in your phone than the person in front of you.
41. **Situationship:** Ah, the most common term in this generation. Nobody really knows what a situationship is, and that is exactly what it means—it's when you are not quite sure what your relationship with someone else is. Your relationship is hanging in the middle with no titles and motives, just confusion.
42. **Slow fade:** Rather than the abrupt ending of things, a slow fade is true to its word. It's when people slowly stop talking until the relationship dies down.
43. **Soft launch:** Introducing your partner by dropping subtle hints on social media.
44. **Stashing:** Do you ever feel like you are someone's dirty little secret? Yep, that's stashing. This is when someone keeps you hidden from their family and friends to avoid commitment.
45. **Submarining:** This too means the resurrection of a ghoster, but this time, they offer you a vague explanation for their disappearance.
46. **Thirst trap:** Posting provocative pictures and videos to attract attention.
47. **Tindstagramming:** In this complex generation, the apps are just as complex as the people using them. This term is used for a situation in which your Tinder is linked to your Instagram and the other person decides to reach out to you directly on Instagram rather than waiting for you to respond on Tinder.
48. **Tuning:** People who flirt like it's second nature to

them while having zero interest in anything else.
49. **Wokefishing:** Pretending to have strong political opinions while, in reality, you don't really care much.
50. **Zombieing:** The resurfacing of a ghoster; they return as if they never left.

References

Admin. (2021, December 15). *Why is forgiveness important in healing?* West Coast Recovery Centers. https://westcoastrecoverycenters.com/why-is-forgiveness-important-in-healing/

Agrawal, V. (2022). How to identify "the gaslight effect." *Robin Stern.* https://robinstern.com/how-to-identify-the-gaslight-effect/

Aislin, R., Mushquash., Jaidyn, K, Charlton., A., Daniel, G., MacIsaac., Kendra, Ryan. (2022). Romance behind the screens: Exploring the role of technoference on intimacy. *Cyberpsychology, Behavior, and Social Networking,* 25(12):814-820. doi: 10.1089/cyber.2022.0068

Amabile, T. M., & Kramer, S. J. (2011). *The power of small wins.* Harvard Business Review. https://hbr.org/2011/05/the-power-of-small-wins

Authentic self-love. (n.d.). Google Books. https://books.google.com.pk/books?hl=en&lr=&id=8VZMDwAAQBAJ&oi=fnd&pg=PA2&dq=Self-Love+Practices+For+Inner+Healing&ots=_UMi4QFzop&sig=QZyEyHxPXJHqLU4kgQtP_sP6m7Q&redir_esc=y#v=onepage&q=Self-Love%20Practices%20For%20Inner%20Healing&f=false

Baskin, T. W., & Enright, R. D. (2004). *Intervention studies on forgiveness: A meta-analysis. Journal of Counseling & Development,* 82(1), 79–90. https://doi.org/10.1002/j.1556-6678.2004.tb00288.x

Bell, N. (2023). How to effectively deal with being ghosted. Counselling Directory. https://www.counselling-directory.org.uk/memberarticles/how-to-effectively-deal-with-being-ghosted

BetterHelp Editorial Team. (2024, March 22). *Online dating and modern relationships in the U.S. | BetterHelp.* https://www.betterhelp.com/advice/relations/the-new-normal-how-online-dating-in-the-us-is-shaping-modern-relationships/

Bijan. (2023, March 9). *Should I block my ex? 21 pros & cons 2024.* Coaching Online. https://www.coaching-online.org/should-i-block-my-ex/

Blackburn, K. G., & Brody, N. (n.d.). *Social media always remembers – which makes moving on from a breakup that much harder.* The Conversation. https://theconversation.com/social-media-always-remembers-which-makes-moving-on-from-a-breakup-that-much-harder-194727

Blackhart, G. C., Fitzpatrick, J., & Williamson, J. (2014). Dispositional factors predicting use of online dating sites and behaviors related to online dating. Computers in Human Behavior, 33, 113-118.

Bosson, J. K., Johnson, A. B., Niederhoffer, K., & Swann, W. B. (2006). *Interpersonal chemistry through negativity: Bonding by sharing negative attitudes about others.*

Conrad, M. (2024, February 20). *What is gaslighting? Examples and how to deal with it.* Forbes Health. https://www.forbes.com/health/mind/what-is-gaslighting/#:~:text=In%20a%20survey%%2020conducted%20by,their%20partner%20or%20ex%2Dpartner

Creus, A. (2014). Digital detox. *COMeIN, 33.* https://doi.org/10.7238/c.n33.1431

Cyr, B.-A., Berman, S. L., & Smith, M. L. (2014). The Role of communication technology in adolescent relationships and identity development. *Child & Youth Care Forum, 44*(1), 79–92. https://doi.org/10.1007/s10566-014-9271-0

DiDonato, T. E. (2001). 4 reasons why people ghost. *Psychology Today.* https://www.psychologytoday.com/us/blog/meet-catch-and-keep/202111/4-reasons-why-people-ghost#:~:text=People%20may%20ghost%20due%20to,view%20ghosting%20as% more%20 acceptable.

Dodson, M. G. (2023, June 21). *Nurturing empathy: the art of thoughtful communication in the digital age.* https://www.linkedin.com/pulse/nurturing-empathy-art-thoughtful-communication-age-mary

Doll, K. (2019). *23 resilience building tools and exercises (+ mental toughness test)*. PositivePsychology.com. https://positivepsychology.com/resilience-activities-exercises/

Estevez, M. (2023). When gaslighting invades our professional, medical and cultural worlds. *Robin Stern*. https://robinstern.com/when-gaslighting-invades-our-professional-medical-and-cultural-worlds/

Faster Capital. (n.d.). *Genuine connections - FasterCapital*. FasterCapital. https://fastercapital.com/startup-topic/Genuine-Connections.html#building-genuine-connections2

Freedman, G., Powell, D. N., Le, B., & Williams, K. D. (2018). Ghosting and destiny: Implicit theories of relationships predict beliefs about ghosting. *Journal of Social and Personal Relationships*, 36(3), 905–924. https://doi.org/10.1177/0265407517748791

Freedman, G., Powell, D. N., Le, B., & Williams, K. D. (2022). Emotional experiences of ghosting. *The Journal of Social Psychology*, 1–20. https://doi.org/10.1080/00224545.2022.2081528

Genie, N. A., & Sharma, N. (2024). Online dating app statistics 2024 - Data driven dating stats. *Nimble Appgenie*. https://www.nimbleappgenie.com/blogs/dating-app-statistics/#:~:text=Statistics%20 Shows%2C%20366%20 Million%20 Dating

Gibbs, J. L., Ellison, N. B., & Heino, R. D. (2006). Self-presentation in online personals: The role of anticipated future interaction, self-disclosure, and perceived success in Internet dating. *Communication Research, 33*(2), 152-177.

Goldman, B. M., & Kernis, M. H. (2002). The role of authenticity in healthy psychological functioning and subjective well-being. *Annals of the American Psychotherapy Association, 5*(6), 18-20.

Goldsmith, O. (1910). *The poems and plays of Oliver Goldsmith*. J.M. Dent & Sons ; New York.

Hamilton, M. (2018). *Emotional resilience: lifebook*. My Identifiers/Thorpe/Bowker.

Hayes, S. C. (2004). Acceptance and commitment therapy, relational frame theory, and the third wave of behavioral and cognitive therapies. *Behavior Therapy, 35*(4), 639–665. https://doi.org/10.1016/s0005-7894(04)80013-3

Healing Holidays. (n.d.). *A guide to self-love & how to practice it | Healing holidays*. HealingHolidays. https://www.healingholidays.com/blog/a-guide-to-self-love

Hitsch, G. J., Hortaçsu, A., & Ariely, D. (2010). What makes you click? —Mate preferences in online dating. *Quantitative Marketing and Economics, 8*(4), 393-427.

Hope Therapy & Counselling Services. (2023, December 12). *Navigating the maze of breadcrumbing in relationships.* Counselling Directory. https://www.counselling-directory.org.uk/memberarticles/navigating-the-maze-of-breadcrumbing-in-relationships

Instagram emoji study. (2016). Quintly. https://www.docdroid.net/6s50RCU/instagramemojistudy20162017-final-pdf

Kallis, R. B. Creating a future relationship or destroying my self-esteem: An exploratory study on dating app experiences and well-being.

Kaye, L., & Schweiger, C. (2023). Are emoji valid indicators of in-the-moment mood? *Computers in Human Behavior*, 107916–107916. https://doi.org/10.1016/j.chb.2023.107916

Kazoun, B. (2018). *Individual growth through forgiveness*: A multiple case study on the process of forgiveness. Walden University ScholarWorks.

Khattar, V., Upadhyay, S., & Navarro, R. (2023). *Young adults' perception of breadcrumbing victimization in dating relationships.* Societies, 13(2), 41. https://doi.org/10.3390/soc13020041

Klein, W., & A Bartz, J. (2023). A historical review of gaslighting: Tracing changing conceptualizations within psychology and psychiatry. *Research Gate.* http://dx.doi.org/10.13140/RG.2.2.30013.23527

Lateefa Rashed Daraj, Mariam Rashid Buhejji, Perlmutter, G., Haitham Jahrami, & Seeman, M. V. (2023). Ghosting: Abandonment in the digital era. *Encyclopedia, 4*(1), 36–45. https://doi.org/10.3390/encyclopedia4010004

LeFebvre, L. E., Allen, M., Rasner, R. D., Garstad, S., Wilms, A., & Parrish, C. (2019). Ghosting in emerging adults' romantic relationships: The digital dissolution disappearance strategy. *Imagination, Cognition and Personality, 39*(2), 125–150. https://doi.org/10.1177/0276236618820519

LeFebvre, L., Blackburn, K., & Brody, N. (2015). Navigating romantic relationships on Facebook: Extending the relationship dissolution model to social networking environments. *Journal of Social and Personal Relationships, 32*(1), 78-98.

Lenhart, A., Smith, A., Anderson, M., Duggan, M., & Perrin, A. (2015). Teens, technology and friendships. *Pew Research Center.* https://www.pewresearch.org/wp-content/uploads/sites/9/2015/08/Teens-and-Friendships-FINAL2.pdf

Lmft, N. A. (2024, March 11). *Breadcrumbing in relationships: What it is & how to deal.* Choosing Therapy. https://www.choosingtherapy.com/breadcrumbing/

Lpc/Mhsp, J. C. M. (2023, September 12). *Dating apps can be stressful, here's how to cope.* Verywell Mind. https://www.verywellmind.com/dealing-with-dating-app-stress-5223900

Maclean, K. (2016). POF survey reveals 80% of millennials have been ghosted! *The Latest Catch.* https://blog.pof.com/2016/03/pof-survey-reveals-80-millennials-ghosted/

Managing social anxiety. (n.d.). Google Books. https://books.google.com.pk/books?hl=en&lr=&id=V8Vys6o0ySoC&oi=fnd&pg=PR13&dq=managing+social+anxiety+disorder&ots=HMd0ys7f3B&sig=lEFkYqJfr94OHzHJhoKTFrH0olw&redir_esc=y#v=onepage&q=managing%20social%20anxiety%20disorder&f=false

Marcello, Russo., Ariane, Ollier-Malaterre., Ellen, Ernst, Kossek., Marc, Ohana. (2018). Boundary management permeability and relationship satisfaction in dual-earner couples: The asymmetrical gender effect. *Frontiers in Psychology,* 9:1723-1723. doi: 10.3389/FPSYG.2018.01723

March, E., Kay, C. S., Dinić, B. M., Wagstaff, D., Beáta Grabovac, & Jonason, P. K. (2023). "It's all in your head": Personality traits and gaslighting tactics in intimate relationships. *Journal of Family Violence.* https://doi.org/10.1007/s10896-023-00582-y

Maurer, D. (2014). The impact of texting on committed

romantic relationships the impact of texting on committed romantic relationships. *Smith College.* https://scholarworks.smith.edu/cgi/viewcontent.cgi?article=1811&context=theses

Miano, P., Bellomare, M., & Genova, V. G. (2021). Personality correlates of gaslighting behaviours in young adults. *Journal of Sexual Aggression, 27*(3), 1–14. https://doi.org/10.1080/13552600.2020.1850893

Michael. (2020). *Gaslighting | Emotional abuse | Stopping gaslighting.* Ananias Foundation. https://www.ananiasfoundation.org/gaslighting/?gad_source=1&gclid=CjwKCAjwte-vBhBFEiwAQSv_xUPTVx1xTlTed2PydzrHznhxcFa95X2W5GpYK75uT4pSdFV5Pa35IRoCzioQAvD_BwE

MSW, D. M. (2022). The mental health effects of ghosting. *Psychology Today.* https://www.psychologytoday.com/us/blog/some-assembly-required/202208/the-mental-health-effects-of-ghosting

Navarro, R., Larrañaga, E., Yubero, S., & Víllora, B. (2020). Psychological correlates of ghosting and breadcrumbing experiences: A preliminary study among adults. *International Journal of Environmental Research and Public Health, 17*(3), 1116. https://doi.org/10.3390/ijerph17031116

Newport Institute Staff. (2024, February 21). *What young

adults want out of dating in 2024. Newport Institute. https://www.newportinstitute.com/resources/mental-health/genuine-connection-in-dating/

Pattemore, C. (2022, May 4). *Breadcrumbing: Understanding why you're being led on.* Psych Central. https://psychcentral.com/relationships/breadcrumbing#breadcrumbing-explained

Powell, D. N., Freedman, G., Williams, K. D., Le, B., & Green, H. (2021). A multi-study examination of attachment and implicit theories of relationships in ghosting experiences. *Journal of Social and Personal Relationships, 38*(7), 2225–2248. https://doi.org/10.1177/02654075211009308

Power, C. (2024, March 18). *Have you experienced 'breadcrumbing' while dating?* Clinton Power + Associates. https://clintonpower.com.au/2017/02/what-is-breadcrumbing/

Prendergast, C. (2023, April 11). "Situationships" and "ghosting": The mental health impacts of undefined relationships. *Forbes Health.* https://www.forbes.com/health/mind/modern-dating-mental-health/

Prendergast, C. (2023, September 28). *Survey reveals 'ghosting' impacts 76% of people who are dating—plus the states with the biggest...* Forbes Health.

https://www.forbes.com/health/mind/modern-dating-mental-health/

Rodríguez, D. G. S. (2020). Gaslighting: How to recognize it and what to say when it happens. *The Psychology Group Fort Lauderdale.* https://thepsychologygroup.com/gaslighting-how-to-recognize-it-and-what-to-say-when-it-happens/

Rogers, K. (2023, December 4). *What is toxic 'breadcrumbing'? Experts share signs and how to address it.* CNN Health. https://edition.cnn.com/2023/12/04/health/what-is-breadcrumbing-meaning-wellness/index.html#:~:text=Breadcrumbing%20refers%20to%20a%20form,are%20not%2C%E2%80%9D%20said%20Dr.

Rosenfeld, M. J., & Thomas, R. J. (2012). Searching for a mate: The rise of the internet as a social intermediary. *American Sociological Review*, 77(4), 523-547.

Sarkis, S. (2017). Gaslighting: Know it, identify it, and protect yourself. *Stephanie Sarkis PhD.* https://stephaniesarkis.com/blog/gaslighting-know-identify-protect/

Schade, L. C., Sandberg, J., Bean, R., Busby, D., & Coyne, S. (2013). Using technology to connect in romantic relationships: Effects on attachment, relationship satisfaction, and stability in emerging adults. *Journal of*

Couple & Relationship Therapy, 12(4), 314–338. https://doi.org/10.1080/15332691.2013.836051

Sharabi, L. L., & Timmermans, E. (2020). Why settle when there are plenty of fish in the sea? Rusbult's investment model applied to online dating. *New Media & Society*, 23(10), 146144482093766. https://doi.org/10.1177/1461444820937660

Silverman, A., Logel, C., & Cohen, G. L. (2013). *Self-affirmation as a deliberate coping strategy: The moderating role of choice.* Journal of Experimental Social Psychology (Print), 49(1), 93–98. https://doi.org/10.1016/j.jesp.2012.08.005

Stern, R. (2007). The gaslight effect. *Morgan Road Books.*

Stutzman, F. D., & Hartzog, W. (2009). Boundary regulation in social media. *SSRN Electronic Journal.* https://doi.org/10.2139/ssrn.1566904

Sumter, S. R., Vandenbosch, L., & Ligtenberg, L. (2017). Love me Tinder: Untangling emerging adults' motivations for using the dating application Tinder. *Telematics and Informatics*, 34(1), 67-78.

Sweet, P. L. (2022). How gaslighting manipulates reality. *Scientific American.* https://www.scientificamerican.com/article/how-gaslighting-manipulates-reality/

SwiftKey emoji report. (2015). Scribd; SwiftKey. https://www.scribd.com/doc/262594751/SwiftKey-Emoji-Report

Tarbert, K. (2001). 5 early warning signs you're being ghosted and what you can do about it. *Features and Health Editor*. https://au.lifestyle.yahoo.com/warning-signs-being-ghosted-what-you-can-do-about-it-expert-advice-232415308

Tartakovsky, M. (2016, May 17). *10 tips for setting boundaries online*. Psych Central. https://psychcentral.com/lib/10-tips-for-setting-boundaries-online#6

Tilchen, J. (2022). *Celebs who were ghosted: Shawn Mendes, Taylor Swift, Miley Cyrus*. J-14. https://www.j-14.com/posts/celebs-who-were-ghosted-shawn-mendes-taylor-swift-miley-cyrus/

Toma, C. L., Hancock, J. T., & Ellison, N. B. (2008). Separating fact from fiction: An examination of deceptive self-presentation in online dating profiles. *Personality and Social Psychology Bulletin, 34*(8), 1023-1036.

Tomshinsky, I. (2013). The art of writing handwriting letters and notes. *International Journal of Business, Humanities, and Technology, 3* (8), 109-116.

Travers, M. (2022). New research helps us cope with the emotional consequences of being "ghosted." *Forbes*.

https://www.forbes.com/sites/traversmark/2022/09/29/new-research-helps-us-cope-with-the-emotional-consequences-of-being-ghosted/?sh=2b21d0c97548

Urban Dictionary: Breadcrumbing. (n.d.). In Urban Dictionary. https://www.urbandictionary.com/define.php?term=Breadcrumbing.

Uncustomary. (2023, December 15). *Dating etiquette in the 21st century: The new rules of romance - uncustomary.* Uncustomary. https://uncustomary.org/dating-etiquette-in-the-21st-century-the-new-rules-of-romance/

Valkenburg, P. M., & Peter, J. (2007). Who visits online dating sites? Exploring some characteristics of online daters. *Cyberpsychology & Behavior*, 10(6), 849-852.

William, A., Klein., Sherry, Li., Suzanne, C., Wood. (2023). A qualitative analysis of gaslighting in romantic relationships. *Personal relationships.* doi: 10.1111/pere.12510

Made in the USA
Columbia, SC
29 June 2024